Flute Solo

FLUTE SOLO

Reflections of a
Trappist Hermit

MATTHEW KELTY

ANDREWS AND McMEEL, INC.
A Universal Press Syndicate Company
KANSAS CITY

Library of Congress Cataloging in Publication Data

Kelty, Matthew.
  Flute solo.

    1. Kelty, Matthew.   2. Trappists in the United
States--Biography.   3. Monastic and religious life.
I. Title.
BX4705.K375A34   271'.125'024 [B]   79-13335
ISBN 0-8362-3912-1

Ave Maris Stella

Contents

1.

Flute Solo

Quite by accident I stumbled onto a happy word in a Greek dictionary, *monaulia*, "flute solo." But it has another definition as well, "the solitary life," since the root word means both "flute" and "house," and the *monos* characterizes the solo flute and the man living alone, the solitary. It is a beautiful combination, for both are a kind of poetry. Certainly neither has any great practical value, yet the world would be less charming for want of the flute, less tolerable if there were no hermits.

I am not a flutist, yet I have a flute and I play it, play it for no purpose and for no ears save God's and my own. That being so, there is no need of artistry or skill and I can sing my tune without fear of correction or disapproval, let alone of another showing me how it should be done. If accomplished play is a good thing, and it is, it is perhaps also true that the way to skill is the end of joyous freedom. It is pleasant and easy to pray by flute and I do much of it. There is some element of pathos in the instrument that is dear to me, something humble and modest in its song. Even when the tune turns out rich and running, there is the sound of the bird in it, clean and selfless. I don't want to learn to play the flute; I prefer it this way. Beyond my incapacity to get far, there is the fear of my small joy being driven away by concern for doing it well and turning a natural act into a performance.

There are those gifted persons who can combine their gift with arduous training and still remain free, a superb accomplishment. Others often cannot, and the pleasure is soon stifled in the achieving. I suppose more persons would sing if they were not so fearful that others would criticize. Perhaps more would pray if they were not so sure it took skill and practice, or be hermits if they were not led to think it out of the question.

Lots of people would like to be able to play something, create a bit of music for themselves. Most want to pray, too. And if not everyone wants to be a solitary, there are not many who have not now and again tasted in lonely hours a solace not elsewhere come by.

We can be talked out of things. Scorn and ridicule are effective weapons and they get considerable use, nor is it only professionals who look with unveiled pity on awkward efforts. Others do so as well. I favor the attitude that permits the child to try his hand at many things, many ways, many times. And the adult.

The solitary runs into a lot of suspicion spoken and

unspoken. It is in the air, an aspect of the climate. People get so that they fear to be alone. Worse, they think it wrong to want to be.

And yet there are so many lonely people. I sometimes feel that's all there are. That we are all solitaries. In a way, it's true. I am the only one of me there is; there could be no solitude greater than that. I came alone. I depart alone. And if I did not exist, nothing else would, even God, as far as I am concerned.

Yet faith tells me that this solitude is not real, that in our aloneness we come from God, are in God, are on the way to God. Further, that we shall one day be one with the one God, so sharing his solitude. Yet that same faith assures us that God's solitude is a community of love. So what looks lone turns out not to be.

Which is why solitude is so good. By means of entering into it, you discover it's not like you were told. It is not lonely in that way. It is lonely, but when you live with it a while, it turns on you, it opens up, it unfolds.

God dwells in the heart of every man, but he dwells there in quiet. He is a very shy God, quiet as a rainbow, and like a rainbow, kin to rain and to sunshine, pointing out hidden gold, sign of a word of promise given after a quarrel, a promise never to be revoked. His presence takes a little while to grow on you, but once the noisy rattling of our tongues, our hands, our head has cleared, one comes to love it. True, there is nothing to see; no word is spoken, no music heard. There is no sweet scent, no subtle influence. What is, is of another kind.

But if you leave it too soon—and everyone will tell you to hurry on, to move on, to come on—if you surrender to guilt and agree with the voices outside, then the heart returns to its old unhappiness, the old fare, the old routine. Yet suffering ever so small a touch of that dark light, it is certain you will return. Do.

Sometimes it helps to do a little something while you are at it, like the flute, as long as it be free and not an exercise. And only for a while, just long enough to taper off the din of a world come in with you. It does not take long. Sometimes a quiet craft, or painting, or drawing. Or the beads. Sometimes a candle will help, a Madonna. Even a bit of incense. Some darkness.

There ought to be a sanctuary, a place where a guilty man could go and know he could not be touched. There ought to be a place to hide, not from the eyes of others, but from my own eyes, too totally centered on what is outside. We need an escape from concern, the eternal fussing and fretting with external. There is an inside to everything and if you know only the outside, then knowledge is schizoid. Most madness comes from living half a life. The best half is within. Or better said, the better half, speaking in terms of the marriage that is you.

It is the dark that gives point to our fears, for in the dark not yet used to, we see too much. The first thing you see on looking into a deep well is your own face and this is at least disconcerting, sometimes annoying. Longer looking reveals what is further down in the well. Even there we are vexed to discover another face which is also ours. Yet, one can grow accustomed to it, and, in a sense, it is a mistake not to, since it, too, is yourself.

Even while you are still with the flute, the past may come up, total recall without pretense, and not always pretty. It is not good to overdo it at first, but you may as well adjust to the fact that there will be more of this.

To want to leave now is understandable, but is still a matter of regret, for you are just on the point of getting to know you. The wise man, instead, would smile quietly, take up the flute again, thinking all the while, musing on it all.

There are places a man can go, a scene he can create, a haven for his heart. The reason they seem scarce is that no one wants them; there is small demand. But lovers always manage to find a place to go where they can be alone for a while. So can you. Playing the flute in public, like love on the street, lacks the grace it should have, the intimate depth.

2.

Venture

The devious route by which one comes directly to what one was meant to be remains as much a puzzle looked back upon as looked forward to. There must be within man some hidden compass that directs him where he is to go. One could easily speak of it as destiny, some prearranged program, did not one feel that it was all accompanied by response, even more by personal choice and election.

The other night I had a dream. I was walking along a wooded path much like a track working its way cross-country here in New Guinea. After some time the path came to a multiple juncture with other paths leading out in several different directions, one much like the other. In the dream I had no notion which path I was to take. I eventually took one and followed it a long way. It brought me to a figure dressed as a bishop who then robed me in priestly vestments of very sumptuous quality.

My dream was very true to life, for if I followed a call
to the priesthood, I have always sensed the fact that it
was as much someone else's doing as my own. I
seemed to follow some instinct in entering a
missionary society, and never once in the course of
long training had I any doubt I was where I belonged.
Before the novitiate was completed I had expressed
my interest in becoming a contemplative monk
several times, but on each occasion was counseled
that there appeared to be nothing to indicate that I
should move in that direction. So I did not, and once
admitted to vows, never considered it again.

Since years later I did become a monk, it is
interesting to reflect on these early desires and the
way everything worked out. There is no doubt that
had I known in my youth about monastic life, that is
what I would have entered upon. At the same time,
from this vantage point, it is clear to me that it was far
better that I did not do so at that time.

There was an introversion to my character that was
pronounced; had it been allowed to develop it is not
likely it would have been healthy. There was much
about life in minor and major seminary in a totally
active order that was contrary to my taste, yet
necessary and good for me. I had to adapt and to
adjust in order to survive, and so cultivated out-going
qualities with zest. I was no good at all in sports; I
think because I did not have the basic aggression
necessary, or, if I did, could not express it in that way.
But there were many other activities and I was
involved in most of them: publications, drama,

music, debate, clubs, and committees. We had endless discussions, arguments, exchanges, and I developed a flair for quick retort and effective ridicule and sarcasm. Since manual labor in that particular era at the seminary was perhaps in higher repute than the intellectual life (World War II was on, labor was short, and we had an open invitation to help on the big farm — a new world to many of us), I managed to acquire some prowess in that, too, and enjoyed working with horses and pigs, in garden and flour mill. In my studies I was about average and had to work hard, not really knowing how to study.

Today, the seminary training that we underwent is looked back on as something depraved and bizarre. True, there was a good deal wrong with it, but at the time, few of us felt so and we took it all in with enthusiasm. There were only a few rumblings of the revolution to come and we did not understand them. We thought of ourselves as competent, alive, and aware—did we not speak forthrightly on such progressive issues as liturgy in English, cooperatives, back-to-the-land and organic farming, indigenous art forms in mission lands? And we looked forward with joy and confidence to the mission work we would be assigned.

There was a great sense of close fraternity in that enclosure which was fostered by almost every factor of the life: a heavy routine of public prayer and liturgy, an almost constant being together, a great sense of sharing in a common ideal. We found it stimulating and we stimulated one another. It occurs to me now that we had innumerable celebrations of one kind or

another: programs or plays or speakers, musicals,
banquets, picnics, get-togethers, hikes, outings,
investitures, professions, ordinations, the cycle of
liturgical feasts. Our time was tightly controlled and
day followed day in spartan discipline. I frankly loved
it and I sensed most of us did. We complained
endlessly about the administration, the faculty, the
prefects of discipline, but that was as much a part of
the life as ritual. And through it all ran a spiritual
current that only added to it and bound it together.

It was a "good seminary" and we were proud of it.
We were further proud to be members of a worldwide
missionary group and felt ourselves superbly blessed
in that. We looked on students in diocesan seminaries
and even in other orders and societies with a kind of
sympathy, quite assured that what they had could not
possibly come up to ours.

It was a fabulous creation, really, and over it hung
some aura of God's and the Church's blessing; it was
divinely right. The tight control that Rome kept on us
was only further proof that evidently we were
important.

Eventually, the whole thing fell apart, though many
years later.

I was appointed to New Guinea and I was pleased.
It was far away, had a romantic appeal, involved a
primitive people I imagined I could relate to more
easily than to some cultured nation like the Japanese.
But the actuality proved something of a disaster. I was
told to assist an older missionary in a bush station. I
entered the work with gusto and was, I believe,
adequate. The scenery was new to me and I enjoyed

the change; making bush trips on horseback, erecting primitive chapels and dwellings. I wrote letters, taught school, gave instructions, baptized and married and anointed, dispensed medicine. And was lonely.

The step from the vigorously outgoing community of the seminary to the quiet life in the bush could not have been more extreme. I had had no contact with solitude for more than a dozen years, and was immediately brought back to the days of my childhood when I much preferred my own company, enjoyed being by myself.

I began to have serious misgivings about my life in New Guinea and grew somewhat frightened. The pastor used to go off on two- or three-week bush trips and I would run the main station while he was gone. When he returned, we would be together a week or so, and then I would take off for my series of outstations and be gone about the same length of time. That is the way we worked. At first we had few books and papers, no radio, no music, no icebox, little European food. We managed well enough, but it was arduous; we expected it to be that way.

But I had not reckoned with loneliness. Sometimes when evening was coming on I could feel a great dark cloud settling on my soul like an oppressive weight. It was much like the rain coming in the night; you could hear it working its way across the jungle, the oncoming roar of torrents beating down on all that rich foliage. I worried, prayed about it. I went to the chapel one night and told the Lord: "You see how things are. You love me. If this is not going to work, get me out of here." With our training and attitudes we would never have asked for a change, certainly not so soon. It was thought proper to ask God, however.

Within ten days of that prayer I received word from my bishop that I had been recalled to the motherhouse in the states to edit the mission magazine of the society. It was the first word I had on the subject. I had been in New Guinea a few months over three years.

Editing the magazine was another thing altogether, but I enjoyed it. In those days we did not concern ourselves with proper training as much as they do today. It was assumed that our seminary had prepared us adequately. Our courses were without number and we had touched on a formidable array of subjects. The assumption was that once ordained you ought to be able to manage as teacher, farm manager, head of a printing plant, a school, a parish, a mission station. By dint of hard work, good luck, and past background, the men did wonderfully well. But there was a lot of bungling. A new superior with new ideas offered me a course in journalism, but along with that I was to edit the magazine and serve as assistant at a local parish. When I saw the extent of the material the course covered, and that much of it would be of no use in my work, I decided not to enroll and settled down to editing the magazine as best I could.

The paper had been begun early in the century as a propaganda piece and means of support and had served the Society well; publication continued until 1960. It was all printed on our own press by the Brothers. As time went on, it became evident that rising costs, new approaches to fund-raising, and the plethora of small Catholic publications were going to force us to call a halt. The halt was called abruptly by a peremptory order from Rome, which is the way things were done in those times. While the last issue was on the press, the plant caught fire at two o'clock one January morning and burned to the ground. I escaped from my quarters only by grace of a kindly Providence.

During the eight years with the magazine my thoughts had often returned to New Guinea and I had an affectionate nostalgia for it. Still, the predominant remembrance was the solitude. I never forgot it; it had left a deep mark.

Meanwhile, community life, as one of the priests of the seminary, was somewhat less than what I had known there as a student. Most of the Fathers were quiet, busy people involved with their classes, their study, their writing, their parochial work. Communal relations were good, but I dearly missed the intensity of the life I had once known. Now and then I preached retreats and enjoyed the work, as I liked helping out in parishes regularly.

Even though I was but dimly aware of it, my life was really falling apart. The New Guinea experience had been a first shattering. As time went on I began to sense something unreal and artificial, something basically untrue and dishonest in the way I lived. My busy, active, outgoing pursuits were somehow not genuine, but put-on, acquired, a sort of pretending. This growing insight really unsettled me. I began to sense a new sort of loneliness and panic.

I sought to make friends among the Fathers and did

so, came to know many of the seminarians, made many deep and lasting friendships. They were a great help to me. Further, I began to enjoy drink, by myself, with others, to a disturbing degree. By the time the magazine was terminated and the press had burned to the ground, I knew I had come to a serious point in my life.

Every now and then the flames of an old love would return and I would again find myself thinking about being a monk. I wondered if that was not what I was supposed to be. I did little or no reading about it, made no inquiries. Once in a while I would meet someone who had just made a retreat at Gethsemani, the Trappist monastery near Louisville, and I would listen to his comments with great attention. I really knew little about the place or the life there—did not even want to know. But the conviction grew that that was where I belonged.

One of my good priest friends died after a long and sad illness. He was dear to me; we used to go fishing together once in a while in the north woods. My situation grew tense and sometimes I did not know what to do. I remember going to his grave one night and, bursting into tears, asking him in God's name to help me. He did.

After the folding of the magazine and the press fire from which I escaped, I had a strange interlude of freedom. I had the conviction that I was at a crossroad in my life and that some sort of resolution was called for. Rather suddenly I decided to make a retreat at Gethsemani. I went with nothing particular in mind, yet I knew instinctively what was going to happen.

The place frightened me thoroughly; completely captivated me. After a few days of fear and indecision, I asked to be admitted to the community. They accepted me, quietly, without fuss, neither much impressed nor unduly remote. It was all matter-of-fact and unexcited. Yet I knew a door had slammed shut behind me.

I returned to the seminary, told them what I had done, asked for permission to enter the abbey. The attitude was one of amusement and incredulity. They assured me of my love for people, for the active life, my talent for preaching, for involvement in works of all kinds. To myself I remarked that they did not know what they were talking about. I typed out a letter to Rome, slipped it under the cloth of the altar of the Virgin for her feast of December 8, then mailed it. The answer was a half-hearted one, but affirmative.

I was getting ready to go, delayed only by previously arranged engagements for some nuns' retreats, when the fire broke out in the press. It was a shocking experience and only emphasized what I had already sensed of the dramatic moment of that period of my life. I injured my foot badly in hot asphalt in escaping from the burning building and it took a while to heal. While the wound was still serious I gave one retreat in Dayton and a second to some novices in northern Wisconsin. While returning from the latter I had another taste of death. The train was racing toward Chicago bright and early that sunny wintry morning, still in the country, when it struck a large truck at a remote crossing. When the train finally stopped and backed up to the scene of the accident, they came to the diner and brought me out into the bitter cold and bitter sight of three bodies flung around the snow and under the twisted wreck. I could smell death and blood while I held one man in my arms as he went into eternity. The second was a young blond in leather boots and leather jacket. I baptized him with melted snow. The third was dead. A long while later an ambulance came and took them away; we got back into the train and went on our way. When we left the train in Chicago I saw the damage done to the front of the locomotive; I felt a worse damage and knew in my heart that I was more afraid of God than ever, remembered cold blood on the snow.

A few days later I left on the night train for Louisville. The evening before we had a social evening in the Father's recreation room and I had all I could get down.

3.

Olive Garden

In the sixties Gethsemani was an intense experience; stepping into it was stepping into an entirely different country. It was death again. My whole identity dissolved and disappeared. At forty-five I had a certain role in life. I knew and was known. I had a history, a community I had grown up with and been associated with on all levels. Once I closed the abbey gate behind me, all that was gone. Here I was not known, meant nothing at all to anyone. The silence that muffled everything immersed me in my nonentity. The place was a maze of complex rites, customs, rituals, modes, and manners that everyone except me seemed to make use of unconsciously, with no effort. There was obviously an intense communication among the group, but it was done mostly by sign language and I knew no sign. January meant that the house was cold, filled with an odor I had never known

before, born of damp wool, incense, and pine-sol. The
dozen or so novices were a varied lot; two priests, a
couple of youngsters just out of high school, some
college graduates, an artist, an engineer, a man from
Ford, and a man from United States Steel. They all
seemed a bit brittle and strained. The novice master
was Thomas Merton (Father Louis); at ease, off-
handish, sharp, somewhat British. It was an ordeal.

The routine had weight. The choir was long and
Latin, complex to stay with, exasperating for one's
desperate efforts to locate proper pages in the huge
volumes; the monks knew much of the office by heart
and were spared the page shuffling. The food was
sparse, generally lukewarm, if not cold, and the
refectory monstrously ugly. The whole complex
looked neglected; the church had needed painting at
least for a decade; most areas needed cleaning. The
grounds surrounding the abbey were nondescript
and the immediate backyard a muddy farmyard every
time it rained. We slept in little cells in an open
dormitory, the air in winter both icy and un-
ashamedly old. Except when doing manual labor, we
were always dressed as monks, exactly how depend-
ing on specific regulations, even at night. And at work
we wore long robes of denim tied around the middle
with a belt, and a scapular or hood. There were all
sorts of distinctions in what postulants, novices,
professed Brothers or professed choir members wore,
and this varied again as to season. At that time we
were still wearing medieval socks, leggings, long
home-fashioned drawers and undershirts. In winter it
was all flannel and wool and one was glad for that.

The novice master was not hesitant about making demands. Every morning after prime and chapter, he would assign us our work. It was rarely the same job two days running. If you could type, you might end up doing some stencils for one of the articles he was working on, and that, often enough, on a bright sunny day when something outdoors would have been a pleasure. On a dark wintry morning with the temperature in the twenties and a stiff wind coming down from Canada, you would as likely as not be sent to clear brush from some exposed patch of pine. Three hours of that after a breakfast of coffee and bread was a good taste of reality.

We had a conference or lecture by the master every day before noon. We always looked forward to it. For one thing, the room was warm. The material was always interesting and Thomas Merton's presentation had great charm. He loved variety. And he had a very kind, gentle spirit in his toughness; he loved good wit and had eyes often merry.

All in all, it was a dreadful period for me. Yet, I loved it, all of it. I was appalled to think the master might find me unacceptable and was almost ecstatic when I learned much later that I was doing all right and would be received. I had a most obnoxious ego, an inflated front, that must have shocked him. He let it pass, taking a good crack at it now and then. Once he came down on me head-first, total-thrust, full-power. I never forgot it. I did not realize what he was about except in the vaguest way, and I did not know how to help myself. He worked on me. He showed me how.

We had interviews with Father Louis every two

weeks or so, for about thirty minutes. They were priceless. He was interested, and even if you thought yourself quite deserving of the interest, he still took you seriously, knew how to guide you. He was very patient. I do not see how he put up with me, so conceited, so cocksure, so thin a veneer of education and pomposity. He used to smile when I would reveal some awareness of what I looked like, and say, "Lots of priests are like that. That's the way they make them."

I learned. I shall never forget him. I am grateful to God for those two-and-a-half years, and for frequent contacts afterward.

As it stated in my request for admission, I went to Gethsemani for a deeper spiritual life, a more intense community life, a life of apostolic prayer. All of which I received in full measure. They delivered.

Yet the greatest gift I had not asked for, had not expected. That gift was an understanding of the role of solitude in monastic life, in man's life. It was Thomas Merton who taught me this, both in the days I was a novice under his direction, as also in later years in a study of his writings. Probably the most significant work of this man lay in his return to the solitary aspect of monasticism. The results of this awakening, this rediscovery, have only begun to be manifest. I am sure it is only a beginning.

It is necessary to see how original he was in this. By reason of his own charisma and his study of early sources of monastic life, he brought back to life this element that had practically disappeared. It was neither easy nor pleasant, for many opposed him.

Thomas Merton was arguing not merely for a revival of the eremitic life within the order, but also for a return to the spirit of solitude which from earliest times had been characteristic of monastic life, of Cistercian life. His writings and studies on this were many and good.

Now, some years after his death and the spreading of his teaching, it is somewhat difficult to recapture the situation on which he dwelt, for Gethsemani has since undergone both an external and internal renovation that is phenomenal. But at that time monastic life there, as at most monasteries of the kind for the past several centuries, had been warped in favor of community. Monks literally did everything in common: their prayer, their work, their reading, their sleep. They were together always. They were rarely, if ever, alone. Together with this intense communal life went silence. Up until a few years ago, there was generally no talk at all, save to a few superiors in governed situations. Even communication by signs was limited by rule. It was this silent community that was conceived as the ideal, and that is the way the monks lived for several generations. Against this backdrop were the protracted sessions in choir, long hours of work—much of it arduous—and times for reading. The tone of discipline was sometimes harsh, even cruel. Yet abbots were known to be kindly, and the way things worked out was to identify strictness with the rule, the life, the order, while the abbot, subject as was anyone else to this rule, did only what he had to do as gently as he might. The combination of a gentle abbot and a tough rule seems to have been accepted as about as good a combination as could be had.

The monks wanted it that way. They were happy men, hard, determined, ascetic, generous. They had what they came for and were pleased. If some were wounded by the regimen, that was not the fault of the regimen.

Merton put his finger on a weak spot. He knew that as long as that weakness was not corrected, all was not well. Monastic life is not just a group of ascetics, men accustomed to hard labor, indifferent to scant food, great stretches of formal prayer and liturgical ceremony, multiple observances and customs in a controlled environment. To some extent it is all that, but that is not the whole of it.

For years, an introduction to the monastic life consisted simply of learning your way around. One did as the others did. Since he considered one element lacking, Merton began to supply it. I believe he felt that when too much emphasis is placed on rigor and hardship, there is likely to be a development of the very sort of ego and false personality that is the basic enemy of growth in God. The regimen often made the monks tough, but toughness does not necessarily equal spirituality. A corps of disciplined ascetics may be an impressive achievement, yet have little to do with monasticism. God may not be able to deal with them.

The monk must first of all be a person made whole by union with his own reality and God's. Too much self can inhibit such union. Merton sensed that what was lacking was solitude. With shrewd insight born of grace and gifted mind, he spent his life proving his thesis and I believe he succeeded. Whether monks will heed his teaching remains to be seen. Rock the boat he surely did; he troubled the waters. Things can no longer be the same.

He did not think that living in a silent community was necessarily an adequate expression of solitude, though this had long been maintained. He thought that a monk needed real solitude; that is, time alone, by himself. And further, and even more important, he needed to be schooled in what to do with that exposure. The greatest lesson Thomas Merton taught me was the fruitful use of solitude.

In this I was helped immeasurably by Carl Jung. I ran into his works in the library—at that time kept in the "reserved" section. I was spellbound by what I read. I still am; I have a dozen volumes of Jung here with me. His understanding of the "way we work" is a great gift to mankind. To my mind, or better, what he has done for me, is to translate ancient monastic teachings into terms I can relate to. They come to life through him.

The other great factors in what understanding I have of what it is to be a monk came through contact with a primitive culture in New Guinea. I am ignorant of anthropology, but even a casual observer can perceive in primitive life a quality that western man singularly lacks; almost everything the native does is religious. If that be too sophisticated, then say that the native lives in two worlds: the world of the visible, the world of the invisible. He is always in touch with another world not of matter. Building a house, making a garden, fashioning a drum, going on a hunt, having a feast, getting married, coming into manhood, going to war—all these and many other activities are always—or used to be before we came —accompanied by ritual, by a mystic aspect, a relation to the spirits. Even if the native's concept of the spirits is not too elevated, even if somewhat limited in tone, the fact remains that to him this world contains much more than we can see. Even if much of this ritualism is concerned with placating inimical spirits, or working out bargains with them, it is contact with a world beyond.

We, on our side, think that the undeveloped nature of the primitive spirit world puts us in a superior position; we know better than to think our ancestors can help our garden grow. We live in a totally material world and fancy ourselves advanced.

Father Louis believed that solitude was essential. He sensed that the discipline involved in exposing self to reality could first of all only be done alone; further, that it ran no risk of developing an ego; that it would lead one to an experience of one's own poverty and sinfulness and thus to a realization of God's mercy; and, thence, to a compassionate love for man. But if this inner journey is not made, one's grasp of one's own being must be grievously limited, with the consequent weakened recognition of God's mercy. Genuine love for neighbor is of one kind with love for one's self and is rooted in reality.

Merton did not indicate anything specific except that permission ought to be extended to monks who expressed some desire for solitude and manifested some aptitude for it. In his own case, he was explicit in his request for a hermitage and was eventually granted it. He lived to see the abbot who for so long found it difficult to adjust solitude to the Cistercian tradition, also established in a handsome hermitage some miles south of the abbey. In Gethsemani, as throughout the order, there has been a revival of interest in the solitary life, and hermits and hermitages are no longer rare.

I certainly had no leaning toward the solitary life when I entered Gethsemani. On the contrary, I felt my need was precisely the opposite; an even more intense community. Nor did I originally respond to Merton's own interest, even though we novices gladly helped ready the ground for his hermitage on the wooded hill. His teaching on solitude impressed me deeply, however, and I found his writings on the subject full of implications for me.

However, in my first years at the abbey, I did manage to find myself a little hut where I could sometimes spend a few hours; these hours meant a great deal to me and were very good. Later I moved into an abandoned pumphouse at the foot of the dam at the end of one of the monastery's many ponds. It was a delightful spot, and though it was damp, I made it into something idyllic. The new abbot permitted me to spend one day and night there each week; also to offer Mass in it.

I can scarcely describe how much the little hut meant to me. At the time, I was in charge of the abbey shoe shop, repairing shoes and providing monks with new shoes, boots, rubbers when they needed them.

Because afternoons were more convenient hours for the monks to come, I worked then and could go for part of the morning to the house near the lake. I got hold of one of the big old Latin psalters and did my office from it, and later acquired from a pawn shop a flute which I used to take with me to the lake (Joyous Lake, I named it) and play, a setting as sweet as I have ever known, since the water is totally surrounded with woods (some of the trees planted by Merton) and to the rear are gentle hills. The echoes from the flute were enchanting. Kentucky is fond of blue mists and a delicate haze often draped everything. Now and then there were wild ducks or a deer. I had the joy of this place several years. I called it Heartbreak House.

It was during these hours that there began to grow in me a longing for a life totally committed to solitude. This development came very slowly, for I much loved the life of the abbey, enjoyed the company of the monks, the liturgy. It always grieved me that some of the monks thought the solitary nursed a grudge against the community. That was not my case; I loved the abbey and still do. It is simply a matter of doing what you feel you must because called to do so.

It seemed to me also that if I was going to be a solitary, it could only be a real solitude if I left the abbey and went some place far away. There is naturally a great advantage in being near the abbey for practical reasons, such as food and clothing, care when sick—even old age and death must be reckoned with. A return on feast days and other occasions would also be a grace. Still, I felt that a solitary ought to bear the brunt of it all and not soften it by settling nearby. But this is only my view.

I began to think of likely places. There are some hermits in Vancouver, for the bishop there offers hospitality, and one needs a bishop's permission. Ireland came to mind, center of monks and hermits years ago, and an abbot there seemed to think it might be possible.

One day, walking out to the hermitage, the idea of New Guinea came to me, so I wrote to a bishop there. I frankly did not expect a positive answer. He is a good missionary bishop, effective, experienced. I assumed he would thank me for my interest, ask for my continued prayers, and conclude it would perhaps be best if I remained in my monastery and as a monk there be a source of blessing for him and his mission.

His answer came back soon enough. He told me to come as soon as I could.

So I went to the abbot. I told him that I had a bishop who not only offered me hospitality, but who also guaranteed to let me live as a solitary, who would help me get settled, and who would also help me in maintaining myself, considering me simply as part of the mission work. We then began a long series of interviews in which I presented my story, the development of my solitary calling over the past years. He listened with an interest that seemed to slacken as time went on. At length I asked him outright if he would permit me to go. He said that he would not.

With that my dream collapsed, for I had long since determined that I would never act on this call without his blessing. As I saw it, if God could give the grace of a solitary vocation to a monk of Gethsemani, he most certainly could inspire the abbot of Gethsemani to cooperate with it. If God chose not to, then the circuit was not complete and I was not about to short it. I had solemnly sworn to obey the abbot and I saw no point whatever in remaining a monk if I were not willing to abide by that. I could always terminate the agreement, but I could not keep it and break it at the same time. So the matter was dropped and life went on as before. What will be, will be, I thought, if God is in it.

4.

Piedmont Interlude

For three years I lived in a small, experimental monastery in the woods of Piedmont in North Carolina, established from Gethsemani. It was a very great grace.

The venture was experimental by reason of its size —no more than six monks—as well as its life. For one thing, the worship was of a very simple nature: psalmody in the night, in the morning, in the evening. Mass followed the morning service. We picked up our own breakfast and supper and took them alone, silently. The meal at noon was in common, a prepared meal, with conversation, although talk at table is not traditional in a Cistercian house. Morning hours were spent in work, mostly to earn a living, but also in doing the necessary chores, since we had goats, chickens, a garden, and woods, and to the running of the place, taking care of guests.

The setting was excellent. A small town was only seven miles away, yet we were sufficiently off by ourselves to assure peace and quiet. While the scene was charming, it was in no sense dramatic. The monastery was made up of a cluster of frame buildings of stained redwood; a chapel, a main building with library, reading room, kitchen, refectory, washroom, and three guest rooms; and six cabins scattered in the adjacent pines for the individual monks, each with one room about twelve feet square serving as bedroom and study. Behind the main buildings was a workshop and at the other end of the property—a rather discordant note—a mobile home.

The mobile home served as a weaving studio. Here we had several floor looms, most of them four harness forty-eight-inch models; one had twenty-four harnesses. We were able to obtain abundant yarn in a local plant from which we wove ponchos and scarves for sale. The proceeds went into maintaining ourselves. We had more or less stumbled into weaving, but it turned out to be a fortunate step. Carolina is arts-and-crafts country, so it fitted in well. Beyond that, there is a certain character to the art of weaving that makes it especially suited to a life of prayer. It is creative and we kept it so, refusing to be tied down to a production of goods that would be the same thing all the time. There is a deep satisfaction in putting on a warp—a long business—and then throwing the shuttle back and forth endless times to form before your eyes, out of conflict and contrast, a pattern and a fabric never seen before. It turns out, as it were, that the material is a construction founded in contradiction, a reconciling of opposites, for the crossing of warp and woof, vertical and horizontal, repeated an infinite number of times, is at the heart of it. Without this cross there is no weaving, and the interplay, always maintained at proper tension and handled with profound respect, was fascinating to work with. Nor were the results predictable. Sometimes the components looked as though they might not blend, but nevertheless combined to create great loveliness.

We joined a craft guild in a neighboring city and took a loom to the annual craft fair where we enjoyed demonstrating. Though weaving in public borders on the irreverent, there was great interest and many visitors lingered to see it being done.

For a long time we kept goats for their milk and learned to respect their remarkable intuition. We kept peacocks and guinea hens for exotica and for taking care that wood ticks did not get too plentiful. A Dalmation taught us devotion.

To the rear of the monastery was an acre of tobacco, leased out, for we were not there long enough to learn how to farm it. And around us was a pine wood through which we cut wandering paths to the main road and mailbox a half mile away.

Usually we made our own bread for table and altar and were even able to get wine for Mass just a few miles away at a small, old-time winery. We ate no meat at the monastery, since this has long been a custom of monks to remind them of nonviolence. It also saved us money.

During our years in the Piedmont there was a great deal of anguish in the country over the war in

Vietnam. Our concern was both with the lack of strong protest from the Catholic Church and the need to stress the monk as a man identified with peace. We felt that many monks were insensitive to the moral implications of genuine patriotism. A lot of discussion led to a small decision: to have the phone removed. We had learned that the phone tax was a specific war tax, and perhaps the only one. Though we could have refused to pay it, we decided to go a step further and dispense with the phone altogether. Doing so turned out to be a blessing. It was sometimes an inconvenience, but we had peace. A six-foot wall around the place would not have assured us more privacy.

We were not entirely shut off, although it is difficult to describe the situation. Large monasteries tend to attract hordes of visitors, and they come for all sorts of reasons. The curious come, as do travelers and people on vacation. They come because they've heard of your cheese or your bread or your farm. They want to hear your chant, witness your liturgy. They are spiritually impoverished and need inspiration. They are lost souls wandering around. They are pious faithful who consider it a matter of pride to be in touch with a contemplative monastery. There are even those who would like to become monks and who come to see what their desire amounts to. Visitors are something of a problem to monasteries, yet, as St. Benedict noted in his rule, you are always going to have them and the abbot should be hospitable.

But the little monastery in the Piedmont was another brand entirely. The liturgy was nothing to see

—starkest simplicity, even rustic—a few figures in cowls, a psalter; it was clear that the cowls covered overalls; over the psaltery one heard the guineas and peacocks on the roof. We had no farm to show, no products save our modest venture in weaving, no great thing in Carolina. One does not go to a monastery to see goats and chickens. And the monks seemed no great species, nor the setting impressive.

Yet people came, from all over, all kinds. We had lots of young people from the universities. Professors came. Jews came. And Protestants. People of no faith at all. Young drifters. Priests came. People from the heart of New York, the woods of Wisconsin, a Swiss, a young man back from monks in India, local Baptists. A dear friend was a church history professor from a small Christian college some miles south; he came often with his students. Seminarians came, Dominicans, Jesuits, Divine Word missionaries, a bishop, a commune-dweller. Most stayed two or three days.

I do not know why they came. Often enough I was there alone, or perhaps with but one or two other monks. Most of the brethren who came there from Gethsemani or other monasteries found it difficult to adjust to the small place, the dominant lonely note, the rural quality of the life, and returned to their abbeys. In the end, after three years, Gethsemani passed the place on to monks of the order from another monastery. They are there at this writing and happy. But people did come. We did not advertise. True, the papers from nearby cities sent out writers and photographers to do feature stories, and we obliged. Our only condition was they were not to

make our location definite, but to keep it vague, that
they mention the horrible state of our road. They
always kept their word. Sometimes the reporters came
back to stay a few days with us. But we never suffered
an avalanche after an item appeared; in fact, very few
came because of a story in the paper.

Yet the word was passed around. One person told
another. Much of the time, then, we had a guest or two
with us; once in a while a larger number. We fit them
into our life and continued as usual. We did not press
anyone, but told them we got up at 3:00 A.M. and
went directly to church. They always came. We put
cowls on them and they took their turns at the psalms.
When the hour was over, they did as we did and
prepared themselves some coffee and toast and took it
in silence. Then there was time to read or pray in one's
cell, or the library, or the chapel. About six we rang
the bell for lauds and Mass. After the thanksgiving
there was a chance for a second cup of coffee, then we
told them what work they could do if they wanted to
help. They always did; some of them were very
handy. At noon we all ate together, chatted, did the
dishes. Then a short nap, after which someone went
down with the dog to get the mail. The afternoon was
free and quiet. No one bothered anyone else and it
was a good time to study, to read, to pray, to work
quietly if you wished, to take a walk. Around six we
had psalms again and found something to eat
afterward—something left over, or some soup or
cereal—and the evening was ours, also in quiet. We
were all asleep by 8:30 or 9:00. The owls and
whippoorwills retired later.

The spirit was one of peace, of love. The place was friendly and warm. There was little tension, no fury. One did not get the feeling of aggression, violence, self-assertion. There was an aura of prayer. Yes, we made God evident; we erected a large wooden cross in the back field; there were shrines in the woods, icons on the walls, pictures, and mottoes. But it was more than a pious place. The place was full of God. He was there before we were.

People loved it. We had little to do with it. God was there. Yet God is as much anywhere as he is there. Maybe men crowd him out. Drive him out, or drown his voice. Mostly in noise, in confusion, in din, in aggression and assertion. Men seem to love fury and fight and angry words and contention. As do men of God. But God runs from such scenes.

Where there is quiet, there is God. And where peace is, and love. If God is dead, we killed him. And we killed him most of all with our noise, the noise of our fuming and agitation. We Americans love violence, but because it is directed against others, it does not lead to the kingdom. I don't think God can stand us. He is afraid of us. He runs away. He hides.

There should be monasteries such as that in the Piedmont all over. Little communities of love. Small clusters of men, of women, of men and women who love peace, who cherish modesty. Small places, disposable places, dispensable—not expensive and impressive layouts. Places a peacock would enjoy, a dog, a dove, guinea hens, goats, sheep. Places where people pray—not elaborate, beautifully tailored prayer, but plain and simple, honest as the psalms.

For the life of me, I do not know why there are not many such centers.

There is but one necessary rule for small groups: adequate time to be alone. We all need space: temporal, psychological, geographical. Togetherness does not breed love. It tends rather to strengthen the notion that the problem is other people. Time to be alone guarantees commerce with God and one's heart; the former the source of all joy, the latter the source of all sorrow.

Monasteries are not out of touch. When a man enters a monastery he takes his heart with him. In coming to know and understand his own heart, in opening it to the Lord to reveal its ills, its poverty, its needs so that the Lord might heal it with his love, the monk is opening the heart of the world. What ails the monk ails everyone else. What ails man, ails him. Why is he any different? He comes from the same place. All the cloister does is open his heart to the mercy of God. And in coming to know his own heart, the monk comes to know the human heart of every man. If a monk is any kind of a monk at all, he will be in touch with his times, not by virtue of *Time* and *Newsweek*, but by his prayer. (Anyway, *The New Yorker* is better).

We all need contact with our hearts. Without that contact we are isolated from truth, divorced from reality. Quiet is certainly one of the ways to that contact. And peace. I suspect seriously that the single most effective weapon of Satan in our times is noise. I cannot think of a better way to alienation and loss of religion. Fill a man day and night with noise, even beautiful noise. Allow him no time to think, to muse, to ponder, to wonder. Fill his air with sound, his ears with din. His heart will die soon enough. Now you have broken him. He can no longer love.

I conclude that it was the quiet peace of the Piedmont house that drew men to it, charmed them, filled them with joy. No one missed phone or radio or TV or stereo. We had a very good library, good papers and magazines, stimulating talks. And lots of quiet.

Once, in our concern for peace, and as a testimony of monastic concern for peace, I mentioned in passing to a peace-activist who was visiting the monastery that I had thought of making a pilgrimage on foot to Washington. I told her that the idea came to me from the custom of the local bishop, who, once each year, led his people on pilgrimages to the Virgin's shrine in that city. It seemed to me fitting that a monk should do the same, but on foot, for the cause of peace. Granted a monk should normally stay home, the gravity of the situation seemed to excuse something unusual, if a pilgrimage be considered unusual for a monk. At the time, peace people were very much discouraged, and she responded with such evident warmth that I could scarcely resist her pleading that I do it.

So I did. I left shortly after midnight on the sixth of August, feast of the Transfiguration, anniversary of the atomic bombing of Japan. My plans were idealistic; I hoped to be able to walk by night and so avoid the heat, carrying a backpack with a small tent, sleeping bag, things for Mass, personal items. Perhaps I should have worn the Trappist habit— white robe and black scapular would have surely been visible—if I was so intent on giving witness, but I feared repercussions from superiors. The actual situation forced me to change things. Night walking turned out to be bad; it was either facing the glare of oncoming headlights or walking the rough shoulders in the dark. The backpack of forty-five pounds proved more than I could manage and after three days I gave that up; perhaps I might have been equal to it had my pace been more leisurely, but there was a distance of 250 miles to cover and I could not be gone too long. I slept a few nights in the tent, a few times in motels, in rectories of parish priests. I reached the outskirts of Washington in twelve days. I think it was a rather foolhardy idea. Highways, even old ones like Route 15, are no place for pedestrians, and the din of passing trucks was especially hard to take at close quarters. I had my Dalmation with me on a leash; she was good company all the way. The summer sun was without mercy, so I had to dispense even with the short scapular I wore as a monk. At the end, a few reporters came out for a story and photos, a meeting arranged by my friend. When I was about half way, she had driven down to meet me to offer encouragement, just as a monk came up from the monastery to bring refreshments and a change of clothes. Once in the city I offered Mass in the National Shrine with a group of Catholics in the peace movement. I had done a bit.

I was rather happy about having made the gesture, and somewhat pleased that I could still manage a good hike at the age of fifty-seven. Once the first two days were over, it was not at all difficult. The monks in other monasteries soon heard of it and were generally sympathetic, even if many had misgivings on how fitting it was for a cloistered monk. I shared their misgivings and understood when no one offered to accompany me when I invited them to do so.

Monks and peace go together. History makes clear that they have sometimes parted company, yet it grieves me that neither the Church nor monastic life is identified with peace, with nonviolence, especially in an age and a country as violent as our own.

The Piedmont was the kind of place that could permit such expressions of concern for peace. Larger monasteries, like institutions, have many aspects to consider, sometimes so many that the only solution to a question seems to be doing nothing at all. Perhaps the bishops as a group were ambiguous by trying too hard to be prudent, for beyond well-known exceptions, the Church's testimony for the Gospel of peace did not amount to much, and even that came late in the day. What action there was on the part of Catholics, and it was both vocal and sizeable, seems almost to have occurred in spite of the bishops.

There is now small point in warming over this recent history, except to indicate that the peace the monk knows in his own heart, in his own community, is not some private garden. Christ builds it, and it is for the monk to share in Christ's work of peace for all mankind. He cannot peer over the wall now and then and exclaim, "Oh, they're fighting again," and let it go at that, certainly not when the fighters assume that the blessing of the monks is with them. Yet, Thomas Merton, as an apostle of peace, was received among his brethren with about the same enthusiasm as by the faithful at large in our land.

It remains true. The monk's basic work for peace is in his being a monk, in his pursuit of peace by the conquest of evil in his own heart. There he touches the whole world. Peace is nowhere if not in the heart; it can take root in no other soil. By grounding his own heart in Christ and his peace, the monk, any man, anywhere, takes the fundamental stand, the basic one, the essential one. It is as such a peacemaker that he is a joy to God and a blessing for the earth, a leaven in the whole mass.

5.

Solsticial Ring

Five years after my original call to the solitary life, the abbot of Gethsemani resigned and we elected a new one. Not long after the latter took his seat, he asked me if I was still interested in becoming a solitary. I told him I was. We started talking about it, and a few months later he and his councilors agreed that I could go to New Guinea to live there alone. It was exactly twenty-five years since I had gone to New Guinea the first time.

Once it was clear to me that the way was open to a life of solitude, there remained only the matter of doing it. Yet, like most doings, this one too needed some symbolic expression which would at once say it and be it in ways both ambiguous and specific. I thought a ring was called for. I looked into the little jewelry shops in the local town and found a simple flat band: it was not silver as I wished, but white gold looked satisfactory and nothing else was available. An engraver inscribed it for me: *O Beata Solitudo* (O Blessed Solitude) on the outside; on the inside: Matthew Kelty—Gethsemani. The man who did the engraving smiled when he was done: "The name is familiar," he said, "I have some of your weaving on my living room wall. Your label is on it."

Then I asked the abbot if he would permit me to make a vow of solitude and put the ring on as testimony. He agreed. So, on June 24, feast of Saint John the Baptist, in the presence of the prior, I knelt before my father in Christ and spoke my vow, following a rite one of the monks put together for me. At the end I pronounced the words: "O Blessed Solitude, with this ring I do thee wed and plight to thee my troth." Then the abbot slipped the ring on my finger and it was done.

The date was fitting. I had made my first commitment to God in the same season thirty-two years earlier. On the very day, the feast of John the Baptist, I made my solemn profession as a monk of Gethsemani. Now, twelve years after that profession, I made my pledge to the solitary life.

John the Baptist has always been a favorite of monks. His feast comes at the time when the sun first begins its journey down. We know this dying will lead to eventual life, and the monk sees in the plunge into night his own way into the darkness of God. The inward journey has all the dressings of death, a decrease, which like death hides the truth of growth in life. John was prelude to Jesus also in this: there is no greater road.

Jesus in word and deed is almost violent in the call for death, for denial, for stripping, for abandoning, for letting go, for leaving all, for the journey up by going down. The monk, almost by instinct, looks to John, first in following after him on this new road. It is the way of contradiction, the endeavor to reconcile what cannot be reconciled. Yet, we all do it, all the time. There is no beat of the heart that does not attest by the very act, a trust that another will follow. Unless we are willing to release the air we hold in our lungs, there can never be a new breath or continued life. The tree must abandon its fruit, the farmer his seed. Each night we lie down to die, sink into the depths with a hope of rising again. We could never let the sun set did we not believe it would reappear. This whole dialogue runs deep in man and all things. One could say, with complete honesty, that life is really no more than a series of heart-breaking good-byes, so full is it of having and letting go, of embracing and parting.

Love, then, is not merely clinging, but also releasing. The womb must unbar its gates, the arms must relax, the fingers unbend. Yet, the faith that makes this possible is the faith that makes life. God often leaves us because He loves us. The monk knows that. John knew it. Jesus left His Mother many times over. He left us all in the end. He does it all the time. Yet his leaving is but the sun going down, the night coming on, the fruit falling from the tree. For the sun will rise, day will return, the fruit fallen and rotten will spring into life.

The ring on my finger bears witness: He will never leave me, not really. And in the emptiness which is solitude, in the wild night of the barren desert, he cannot hide from me. And even if the sun should never rise and the night be without end, I will still believe, even if I wait for all eternity. Though he never answer, I will yet knock, and knock again. He fools me not; I am wise to him. I know him. I know he loves me, so I do not care what he does. And in life without care, what joy of heart!

And in any case, here in the tropics and south of the equator, everything is something else again, for here, come June 24, the sun begins to rise, not sink, it is the way up, not down. Which is what I have been saying all along.

6.

Sea Route

It seemed best not to make my journey to a hermitage in New Guinea too hasty. Speed would not have been an appropriate note with which to approach such a life, and I had no desire at all to jet here. It had to be by sea, but booking a passage was not so simple as I had imagined. Freighters looked ideal; luxury liners not. Yet the paucity of liners had made berths on freighters very hard to find. It was by way of another's cancellation that I sailed out of New York in November on a new container-cargo vessel of the Farrell lines bound for Sydney via the Panama Canal.

It was a good trip on a good ship. Once under way, we made but one stop, at Panama, twenty-two days in all. The Pacific is a mighty sea and we had ample time to attest to that. We were twelve passengers, mostly retired people, lovers of the sea. Ship life was quiet and restrained, the officers and crew friendly enough.

The ship was much like a monastery. There was good enclosure, better than the best of cloister walls. The captain made a worthy abbot, nor was a prior wanting, a subprior. Obedience was evident in practice, devotion to duty, to labor. The ship was no less on a journey than any monastery, and the presence of God was not subtle. True, there was no explicit praise of God, as one finds in every group of monks, yet his praise was there and I heard it. Men of the sea live close to God.

As Saint Benedict notes in his rule, guests were not lacking, and as the same rule provides, we were hospitably received by the abbot; yet, like guests in any abbey, were something of a jarring note to officers and men. We were alien and a distraction, full of silly questions; a disturbance, and a lot of work. I dare say they would sooner have had the ship to themselves, nor would I blame them. Over everything hung that same sense of unity that marks any monastic group, a being thrust together by some destiny that for a time made us one small world, one more solitary. We might just as well have been a lone mariner on a raft.

I caught myself calling the master an abbot, so close was the resemblance, nor was I far wide of the mark; he would have made a good one. Family life was wanting and, as in a monastery, wives and children were not part of the scene, save among the guests — another factor that set the passengers apart.

Some think monasteries unusual and artificial. Rather, I find them as common and natural as a Greyhound bus crossing Kansas, or a subway crossing town, not to say a ship at sea.

There is no denying that the sea is a good metaphor of God. Its majesty and power stagger the mind of man. For the most part, this voyage was one of fair, mild weather, yet anyone who knows the Pacific knows its gift for violence and treachery. The sea can be cruel, relentless, without remorse or regret.

God is strangely like the sea. His ways are beyond fathoming, as was said long ago. Faith tells us of God's goodness and mercy; we believe. Yet, there is evil in the world; call it real, call it apparent. Nor is the world tidy. Innocent folk suffer much. Apart from death itself—no minor exception—there is much misery, most of it seemingly needless. There is no human being alive who cannot, from the brief span of his years and experience, relate an imposing number of tragedies that have touched those near to him, known to him. When one considers the world at large and its day-to-day story, one is stunned by the amount of suffering that exists. And even our own limited knowledge of history is one full of wretchedness for untold legions.

In the face of such a long-standing catastrophe one is hard pressed to sustain a faith in God's mercy and love. And most people have met individuals who have categorically rejected faith in God because of the very presence of so much evil about which he seems to do nothing.

It is always disturbing to meet fine people, blessed in mind and body and the goods of this earth, and after coming to know them more intimately, learn that sorrow and suffering have touched them, God's finger. One comes to realize, eventually, that all human life sometimes falls in his shadow, often dreadfully.

Spending hours looking out over the sea, I could not help telling her, "How beautiful you are! What a glory is yours! By day, by night, by moonlight, at sunrise and at sunset, what magnificence. But, ah, you treacherous one! I do not trust you. You would turn on me in a moment. You would gladly, happily devour me, and should the mood seize you, could so easily batter and beat this mighty vessel as to leave it a sinking shambles." ✓

And yet the sea is like God. God is like the sea. Is it fair to say that? Proper? I do not know. I see God only as he comes to us. I realize in faith that God is supreme goodness and beauty. And I also realize that this is his world, that he sustains it and keeps it in being, that nothing happens without his knowledge and permission. I know his almighty will governs all things.

Yet, in the face of evil and the effects of evil, one is helpless. Only faith can sustain one.

Some priests stopped at the monastery one day and in the course of the conversation, the matter of evil, the devil, came up. They asked me if I believed in the devil, since I had already several times mentioned him. I said that I did, of course I did. It turned out that they did not, that they did not personify evil, that they considered this an attitude of more primitive times, that they believed all evil came out of the heart of man.

Perhaps. To be sure, all that fits more easily with our thinking, but it does not do much to answer the question of evil in the first place, and how it got into the heart of man. And one has to juggle Scripture very considerably to dismiss the devil, Satan.

For the moment I shall keep my belief in the devil. He is no great problem for me. His works are manifest. It is certainly just as easy, if not easier, to believe in the devil as in God. True enough, one needs grace to believe in God. We know Satan by his works, and they are all around us, in us.

The test of faith comes not so much in belief in God or belief in the devil as in God's toleration of evil. Why has he not banished evil from the earth? Or why has he not banished it from the hearts of men? I assume he does not will to because we do not want him to do so.

Evil does not float around in space. It is present only in the hearts of men. The evil that we experience in nature—in fire and wind and water—is a reaction to man's heart, a reflection of basic disorder and a desire to restore order. All things are tied together and when man's heart is not right, nothing is.

I have no doubt whatever that when the hearts of men are all renewed in Christ, the world itself will be renewed. But so long as evil abides in a human heart, evil is present on the earth and the earth will resist it.

Belief in Satan is not a projection outside myself, a convenient way of unloading my own guilt, my own evil. It is rather to postulate its source, the presence that my own heart shares insofar as it is allied to evil. The community of evil is some sort of union binding all who will to be so bound, affecting all hearts and the world we live in. Not to believe in this source and inspiration is simply to ignore the root because it is below the ground. It neither answers the problem nor disturbs it. It passes it by.

But faith also tells us that Christ has vanquished
Satan and conquered hell and death. This means that
despite the alarming impact that evil obviously has on
the world and on me, its power is deceptive. Further,
that the very pain, suffering, and death that men
know, themselves become instruments of redemption
for all mankind by virtue of Christ's undergoing them
with us and for us. If Christ has known not merely
human life and labor, human joy and happiness, but
also human suffering and human death, then everything that Christ touched of life and labor, joy and
happiness, suffering and death, has now been given a
new character and a new quality.

The world has not changed much since Christ came.
Things are pretty much the same. There are still
earthquakes and cyclones and floods and famines.
There is crime in high places and low. There is pain
and death in every human family. The scene is not
really all that different.

Yet, there is a difference. A total difference. Into
that human maelstrom a divine life has been thrown
which deprives evil of all its real power. What had led
men to despair, to hatred of God, and most especially
to love of evil, now can lead man to salvation, his own
and that of the whole human family.

The Christian's response to evil is thus dynamic. He
does what he can to avoid it, but when it comes his
way in whatever form, he is not overwhelmed by it,
but rather overwhelms it in the grace of Christ, makes
of the very suffering the road to joy.

I rather feel that all men will be saved. It is at least
possible that in the interval between life and death,

before one steps into eternity, such light and grace may be given a man as to enable him to reject all evil, turn to God and goodness. I am particularly encouraged so to think in the face of so much suffering on the part of the innocent, of children.

The saints all embraced suffering, accepted it, bore it humbly for Christ and with him, in him. In so doing they aligned themselves with him in the salvation of humankind. Beyond the known saints, how many uncounted good men and women have borne pain for Christ's sake and so shared in his passion for man.

And beyond the end effect of participation in the ultimate triumph of good in the kingdom of heaven, the bearing of pain with Christ in this life is the greatest good we can do toward establishing the reign of Christ on earth, since such action removes the venom from suffering and turns it into a vessel of grace. It follows that the more hearts there are ennobled by grace, who enter on his way of pain to diminish the power of evil, the more quickly the end of evil on earth is brought about. It turns out, then, that union with Christ on his cross is the most fruitful means of hastening the coming of his kingdom. It is such a wisdom that led saints voluntarily to enter into suffering, pain, and death.

If evil is totally removed from the hearts of men, how could it be that nature would continue to revolt against man, and not instead reflect the goodness manifest there? We know from many legends of the holy men and women of God how animals responded to them with unwonted tenderness and affection, even animals otherwise violent. Such stories ought not to be dismissed too easily. Most of them are probably genuine.

Evil is a great mystery and manifests some great primeval conflict of which we know little save the results. We know, too, that through the ages the minds of men have struggled with this problem, a struggle that continues down to the simplest person on earth suddenly struck with catastrophe.

Job is a most excellent book, full of good food, pondering matter. The ancient problem of suffering innocence is there probed at length. We have the ultimate and most pertinent example of the innocent suffering in Christ, and know that in Christ's answer lies ours.

Our suffering, as often as not, has small relation to personal guilt. We are a guilty race and as such we suffer. Our guilt is communal, as is our suffering, and it is this very communal aspect that enables us to rise in faith to the awareness of our capacity to share in Christ's saving work for our brothers. We go to heaven together. Nothing is lost. Nothing wasted. The share that is ours does not, indeed, win heaven nor earn it, nor is it even necessary—anymore than Christ's passion and death were necessary. They were not. One word from Christ could have redeemed the world, but the Father's will was other. We can conclude that our suffering, too, is not necessary, but is in the Father's will. If we submit to the will of the Father, we submit to it in Christ and with Christ. Christ's agony in the garden was a complaint we may one day make our own if the Father's hand lies heavy on us and he permits Satan to buffet us. But in such submission we make possible our own share in glory, not ours merely, but a sharing by all.

There are not two principles in the world, one good and one evil. There are not two gods, one the Lord God, the other Satan. There is but one principle: good. There is but one God: the Lord. But the Lord God who is good is opposed, and this opposition is the existence of evil, personal evil. Further, this evil power was permitted to tempt man, and to this temptation man succumbed. Man has since suffered the consequences of that sin, in his own heart, in the hearts of all men, in the world around us.

Christ has entered into our human scene, become one of us, shared everything we have save evil, a gift we could not offer him nor he accept, since he is pure good. But he drives evil from our hearts if we will have him do so; he invites us to follow him in his bearing of suffering and death for others that the power of evil may be totally vanquished. The Christian is one who has received Christ into his heart and so is free of evil, possessed by the Good Spirit; one who freely takes on whatever suffering God's will presents, out of love for him and the brethren.

The many who suffer and die without awareness of Christ and his mercy do not suffer and die apart from Him, we might think, but share in his work even if they are not aware of it. Certainly, the Christian so prays as an expression of his vocation in the world: a conscious participation in the Redemption, a conscious entry into the conflict with evil, its conquest.

There is no question that evil is a great power and that suffering and death are most potent weapons in stimulating hatred for God, love of evil, despair. Further, we know that evil breeds evil, as violence breeds violence, crime breeds crime. Satan need never manifest himself, but simply permit the works of darkness to proliferate. Our enemy, then, is the evil one, to be driven first of all from our hearts, from the hearts of all men, by Christ. The willing acceptance of suffering is, of all, most noble among the marks of the man of God, since it so perfectly relives Christ in his forebearance, nonviolence, nonresistance, patience, submission. The way of this world is flight from pain, refusal to bear wrong, rejection of suffering, hatred of death: a code of evil for evil, violence for violence; revenge, retaliation. The willing acceptance of voluntary deprivation and pain for the sake of the kingdom is the mark of the Christian.

The sea beats itself against a coral shore here at my door in New Guinea as it has been doing through countless ages. "Great sea, symbol of eternity on whose shores Christ stands and waits! Someday you will lose your cruel heart, you will be softened and made benevolent, no longer hostile to the human. Once our hearts are all renewed in Christ, you will be so rapt by their beauty that you will treat us all tenderly. On that day you will gladly support us when we walk on your waves. And should you become rough and unruly, one word from any of us will calm your waters, for you will willingly hear the sons of God."

The sea can wait, they tell us. Yes, and has been waiting, a long time.

7.

New Guinea

The bishop suggested a hilltop here in Bogia as a site for my hermitage, the setting of the mission station before World War II. Since the missionaries' time on the hill had covered over forty years, it is likely to be well-equipped and attractive. The missionaries all remained when the Japanese forces overran the island and, although put under house arrest early enough, were decently treated until the tide of the war turned. Once that trend set in, brutality and cruelty became the rule and eventually they were either exposed to death or simply put to death. Over 150 of them were so to perish, including bishops, priests, Brothers, Sisters. And before all was over, little of the chain of mission stations along the coast, including the headquarters and cathedral near Madang, was left standing. The hilltop in Bogia was bombed bare.

When the missionaries returned here after the

disaster, they decided to settle on the shore at the edge of the coconut plantation, even though that meant giving up the splendid view, the breeze. The people had grumbled about the arduous climb.

A complete station has been built down on the coast: church, rectory, guest house, convent, many classrooms, houses for teachers, store, workshop. There is a decent wharf, storage sheds, house for the plantation manager, garage. The total is no doubt more impressive than the former complex, though the old one was more conspicuous; the church tower was visible far out to sea.

My reaction to the bishop's suggestion was hearty; I liked the idea very much. For one thing, I was concerned about being assigned a bush station in a rather remote area that had become somewhat depopulated. There has been considerable movement of the people closer to the shore road and also to the towns. The road means access to stores, to work, to government centers, to the open market. Yet, the departure of many does not leave a village empty; the places are not abandoned, and former inhabitants return frequently to look after gardens and houses, to keep in touch. My being given a house in such a situation would thus involve me in mission work and, as a monk, I had not come here for that. This had already been agreed to before I came, was a condition made essential by my abbot. It is true, I would not have objected to some modest involvement, but the dimensions that modesty suggests are not precise. It would be simpler to have no ministry at all.

This approach put my role in rather strong terms,

and I was aware of that. On the other hand, I had made no effort to ascribe to my coming here any practical value. The monk, the monastery, has no evident use. The uses they do have and have had are not an essential aspect. If monks of past ages have been agents in the preservation or furthering of art and culture, a civilizing influence, this is not their prime role. True enough, guests of an abbey are generally impressed, but the impression is as likely as not to be a reflection of their own values. Monks are not too moved by praise of their skill in agriculture or art or manufacture or even liturgy; even, if the facts warrant it, for being men of peace and love. The monk lives for God. Any appraisal of his life that is not referred directly to God is in some way impertinent. I suppose the ideal monk would be unknown to anyone and therefore not subject to human judgment.

To come to a mission land, then, where the life of the Church is evident in a vast ensemble of activities carried on by zealous workers for the kingdom of God, with nothing further in mind than prayer on a hilltop, some work in a garden or in the woods, some reading and study, hours of psalmody—all in a setting removed from day-to-day life—is bound to raise some serious questions. I see no way of avoiding that.

The monk's vocation is in his emphatic dedication to the praise of God, the study of God, the awareness of God. This is to deal with a set of values other than the works of mercy, though not to set them aside. No one ever said that the monk's life was total Christianity, nor the perfect following of Christ, nor the model for all. It is a misunderstanding to construe the

monk as the ideal Christian or to endeavor to fit him
into such a frame.

The monk gives body to one aspect of the Christian
life, and that is prayer, particularly prayer in solitude.
The monk is with Christ on the mountain alone at
night, he is with Christ in the forty days in the desert,
in the garden of Gethsemani, in the hidden years. But
he is not his companion in the ministry, in his
preaching the word of God, in the healing, in his
miracles, or even in his passion and death. The Christ
at prayer is the monk's Christ and everything follows
from that, though what follows may well include
ministry, preaching, miracles, passion and death,
should God so will.

No one can follow Christ in everything, but one can
follow Christ with a particular attention to an aspect of
his life. Without doubt, most Christians follow him in
the hidden life, not the public one. Some are put to
death with him and for him. Some preach his word.
Some heal. Some minister. Most pray, at least at
times. Practically all Christians, though, work for a
living in the bosom of a family love, and follow Christ
in those very years to which he gave most of his life.

It is true, we do not take Christ apart; that we follow
Him, not a portion of him. Christ is whole and cannot
be divided. Yet, in our accompanying him we are
with Him sometimes visibly and sometimes not, most
often not. For all that, we are with him incarnate,
working, preaching, praying, healing, condemned,
dying, rising, and ascending to glory. Very few,
perhaps no one except the Mother of our Lord, knew
him from the beginning to the end. Even those who

were intimately associated with him were close to him only for a brief time, and even among them, some more briefly than others. Those who walked in his ways then, now, and all through the centuries have been beyond all counting, as have their manners of doing so.

The service of Christ cannot possibly be tied down to one or the other or several as more appropriate. One does what one is called to. One does what one can. The basic call is to holiness, and holiness like Christianity, can be found anywhere, works anywhere. It had just better, for if we are going to wait until the world is fit to live in, we may be a long time waiting. It is better, it seems to me, to do what we can with what we have, and make the best of it. It is possible that our sanctification lies in precisely that, not in a better world that never arrives.

In being a monk, I assert my right to be myself and to do as I see fit. Or more aptly, to do as God wants me to do. Or more practically, to do the only thing I am able to do. Even if I choose to do nothing, who is to correct me? Anyone with eyes to see is aware that most human action has its element of corruption, that often what is done for the glory of God is heavy on glory and light on God. I fail to be unduly impressed with action and I use pragmatic norms in arriving at that impression; the results justify it. What goes on in the heart seems to me at least as important. Privately, I think it is more important.

Christ did nothing worthwhile for thirty years. One carpenter more or less in Nazareth could scarcely have mattered. For all practical purposes, they were wasted years. And it is precisely to that kind of waste most men are called. And even within the scope of his few public years, Christ was wont to waste further time by running off to the hills when there was work to be done. Even in the few years he did apostolic work, as we call it, he reached few, healed fewer, and in the end succeeded only in raising so much opposition and ill-will that they put him to death.

In all of that I see no justification whatever for the notion that work for God necessarily means a life of feverish action, back-breaking labor, constant tension and concern. This may lead only to mental, physical, and spiritual exhaustion. Neither the plan nor the result seems Christian. It may perhaps be no more than Western aggression and drive transferred to religion. It is more horrible to look at there than elsewhere.

Men of God are thus not necessarily all that concerned with God for reason of much bustle. They may be, but it is not the bustle that proves it. The lack of this bluster, then, can scarcely be said to be the issue, or the presence of it. Or, simply, what we do matters very little. It is not where the action really is.

God is still God. I have been on earth almost sixty years and over two-thirds of that time in his official service and I don't even know him. I've not begun to begin to understand him, to relate to him. I've spent half a lifetime doing what they told me to do, pouring myself out in a frenzied effort to produce, to deliver, to come up with results. The total result of all this seems, in terms of anything that can be measured, a zero.

And in terms of my own inner fruit, the same: nothing.

Take your good works and be gone with them. I'll take my flute, the stars at night, my few books, the psalms. I'll manage somehow. And if I am forced to, I'll not hesitate to come beg an alms from you. In any case, I feel I was an arrogant monster full of ego, determined to provide salvation by dint of projects and programs of every sort. I've had enough for the simple reason that God was a diminishing factor in all of it. I am now headed in the opposite direction and have sworn to stay with it. I do not know whether I have found God, but I have found peace.

The bishop is all for it. He has given me this hilltop with the glorious view and has promised me a little house: two rooms, one a chapel, one to live in. Surely the most impressive feature is the water tank to hold the rain falling on the corrugated iron roof.

A sundial is on the way. We had one at the Carolina monastery, set up for a remembrance of the bishop's visit there two years ago. He blessed it during the rainy aftermath of a hurricane on the feast of Saint John the Baptist, summer solstice. I am hoping he will be able to come bless this house on the hill on the same feast this year, blessing the sundial too—our symbolic link with the cosmos. The day would be appropriate, for John the Baptist is a patron of monks.

Meanwhile I have a small cottage down here at the edge of the mission compound and manage well enough. I take my meals with the group, no monk's fare, but plain enough. For the rest, I have spent time on the hill, clearing it of jungle with the help of four local men from the area I used to work in years ago. The spot now looks ready. I follow the routine we had at the little monastery and find the psalms more apropos than ever in this new situation. The sea is at my door, the surf a persistent background, and around me lots of coconut palms, especially picturesque in these past nights of the paschal moon.

Each passing hour of the day is another kind of beauty, for the sun here is astonishingly bright and all colors most intense. Through the palms I see Manam, a volcanic island twelve miles to sea. Occasionally she spouts dark fumes from her depths, secrets from her heart that drift still unrevealed across the sky. The shoreline is a series of low hills, some wooded, some grassy, with palms along the beach. There is generally a soft mist in distant scenes, and rain clouds seem always to be gathering or scattering in some area of the sky. Now and then they come over, drench everything, and pass on to give the sun domain. The whole scene, in fact, is so moving that I wonder if I am not too handsomely set. And the top of the hill is still more of a spell.

I do not know what will come of it all. I really do not care one way or other. Possibly some of the people here will be interested; maybe not. It does not really matter. There are no other monks in New Guinea, though there are contemplative nuns up the coast at Aitape and also in Port Moresby, but their convents are impressive.

No one could know at this juncture, but it does strike me that coming alone may have been wiser than I thought. Had a group come, even a small one, they would have been more acceptable. In no time at all they would have built a respectable monastery, probably with library and guest house, and set up some form of income—industry, such as a cocoa or coffee plantation, a craft of one kind or other, a dairy herd for butter to sell—all bound to confirm everyone in the opinion that these monks had their feet on the ground and knew what they were doing. Which is to say, the whole thing would have made a bad beginning. One man, without resources, unable to throw weight because he has none, may be taken less seriously, but the emphasis on prayer and solitude will be there, and if that raises questions, the questions are at least relevant.

The primitive lives in a world open to the spirit, and my suspicions are that monastic life will mean much to him—though a monastic life adapted to climate and culture, preferably lived in solitude. Solitude is not, I believe, a common element among them, nor even appreciated: the loner is often feared as one possibly endowed with superior magical powers; but a secluded community of men given to a life of prayer, simple labor, reading, might be a form of life they would find appealing. The Western Church has inadequate outlets for the mystical here too, so an opening in the way of the contemplative life appears called for. Perhaps it is too soon. That would not distress me. I feel God has called me here, so I shall simply live as a monk, and sowing that seed, let come of it what may, now or later. Personally, I have no desire whatever to lead a community, let alone found one, but if that is God's will, perhaps I could adjust to it until someone else comes along.

Out on a reach of the hill to the rear of my place is a small cemetery, almost completely invisible for overgrowth. We cleared it enough to be able to get to it and about in it. There are two Fathers, three Brothers, two Sisters buried there, going back to 1904. Three of them lasted but one year in New Guinea; in those days blackwater fever was a menance and many succumbed. I have company on the hill, thus, and find a certain comfort in their presence and in our assured relation in God.

I am not the first Cistercian in the area. Monks from an abbey in eastern Europe were here at the turn of the century with a view to founding a house. One of them was killed in neighboring New Britain in a native uprising and that seems to have been the end of the project. I would hope my venture comes to a different term, yet God leads us in odd ways, not loath to beckon us down blind alleys and up dead ends, but there is wisdom in his madness. A certain wry trust and bemused tolerance are called for in order to keep the heart light and the steps free. In the end, all will come out well, just as the lady said in Norwich a long time ago.

8.

One Way

Almost anything can be a way to prayer. Like a motorcycle. I am not sure this is one of the recommended methods, but it is for a person to learn for himself what best leads him to God.

What is it about a motorcycle? Surely not the noise (they need not be used that noisily). Nor the power. Nor even the expense. It is more than a matter of gas economy and quick, easy transport. No, there is some mystic dimension that escapes no one. There is a fascination in a motorcycle that has deep roots. It surely has something to do with solitude. It is obviously related to the matter of journey, of pilgrimage. There is some quality of exposure, of risk, of total commitment that is evident to a remarkable degree in this medium.

It was a long time coming for me, for conditions made it altogether impossible. But one day everything fell together and I was mounted.

Is this a good way to make love? I do not know. I know only that for me it was. I have long tried to discover why it was so, and do not yet really understand. If I do not know myself, it would follow that I could not understand why I do the things I do. But there are things we do, even when we do not know why, that we feel to our depths are right. One knows when one is in love.

Not in love with a motorcycle, but in love. There is palpable poetry here, so evident that I am sure someone somewhere must have written of it. But I have never read of what I know.

What is it about leather? Again, I do not know. I managed not merely leather boots, but leather jeans (white) and shirt and jacket as well; and helmet and gloves. Is it wrong to feel they were vesture?

There are motorcyclists, I know, who never seem to go anywhere and do little more than roar around a certain neighborhood. And I know, too, there are unsavory groups who frequent highways in some locales. And there are those small bands who travel together, those who gather for racing or cross-country cycling of a hazardous nature as a form of sport or competition. But my man is that lone cyclist one passes on the road now and then. I think he is the one closest to the secret of it all.

What is it about going down the road alone, open to wind and weather, up and down hills, around sweeping curves, so free, yet so much disciplined to a skill that makes the whole enterprise a magnificent form of play? The play that prayer is kin to. There can be little to compare with a lonely night in the rain, with lightning sometimes breaking the sky, distant thunder rumbling over the drone of your motor. Can anything equal the passage through mists in the mountains by night, riding into the chill dawn, the rising sun?

It is not that you see so much beauty—the sea, the dangerous bridges, the rolling country—but that you are part of it, share in it. You are not shielded from it, removed from its influence and impact. The wind pressing your clothes tight to your body, the life of the engine between your legs, the quivering meeting of the wheels and the road—all of it together releases some song of joy from the heart in a liturgy of thanks. Song on the way, thanksgiving for life.

For it is true, we journey. There is not one of us who is not on his way. We know when the trip began, we do not know when it will end. Nor do we know where it will lead us, what we will encounter on the way. We do know, in faith, whence we come, and, please God, where we go. We know that on the way his word and his sacrament sustain us, keep us going. We know that often the road is difficult, sometimes impossible, just as we know it is sometimes pleasant, happy. We know, too, that it is a communal journey, a community pilgrimage to some Holy City. We are all making it, we are all making it together. Even though I am all alone on the back of my machine, my solitude is shared by all. I am no more alone than anyone else, no one more lonely than I am.

What is that wholeness that makes man one flesh? There are many forms of union, but the ultimate union is that totality of all that I am, that oneness of soul and body that is an image of the union to come, in which God and I are one. There is no earthly love that does not in some way describe the whole that every man is called to, is not again symbolic of the nuptials to come in which God and I will be wed.

And that marriage will be the union of all mankind in God, a community of love in which we will both disappear and find ourselves. There is no love in which one would not gladly die, be totally submerged, no love in which I would not all the same be, and be forever.

The lone cyclist on the road is not alone at all. He is one man of the community of the lone on their way to the King's City. His loneness is a seeming one, no more real than is the community created by a gathering of people in a coliseum. Love makes one whole and when one is whole, one is united to all. It is in the depths of the heart that we discover not only our own humanity, but all human nature and humankind.

There is some spouse within we must meet, and failing that, fail wholeness. It is not enough to be charitable, to be busy in the works of love, however splendid and generous. There is in the heart of us all some image of the Beloved we must not merely acknowledge, but know, love, embrace. Without this marriage there can be no real human life. Man was not born to live alone.

But this is a mystic love, not a carnal one, a love born of poetry and music, nurtured by tenderness and compassion. Yet it is a love won only at terrifying cost and hard labor. There is an exploit involved here which is of greater import than any external act. Indeed, the external act can have small value unless it be transferred to the inner scene and made effective thus.

The meeting of the bride within is not had merely for the asking. Her hand must be won; love of her must be proven. Heroic effort is taken as a matter of course. She dwells beyond dark mountains and deep abysses, dangerous and difficult to cross.

Notwithstanding, many find her, and these are the people who have truly lived. It is these who know God and who will see his face because they know what love is. The mystery of life is in winning the beloved and union with her, for in their union one discovers God.

Why is it so difficult? Why should it be so heavy a labor to find God, know love?

I would suppose because we are so timid. We are fearful, fearful most of all of the truth. It is the truth that shall make us free, but at that price many would rather not be free.

We can be redeemed only if we want to be and no one will want redemption unless he knows how much in need of it he is. But one will never know this unless he is willing to look at his own face and into his own heart. And that is the reason men fear silence. And quiet. And solitude. For in that light they see light. And seeing it, take flight, sometimes excusing themselves, often not.

And that is why you take the Gospels with you on your motorcycle, for in the Gospels we meet mercy. And it is Christ's mercy that encourages us to be unafraid of darkness, of rain, of storm, of mist and mountain. Or the face of evil.

No one looking into his own heart will do so long before confronting not merely evil, but the power of evil. No one knows his own truth unless he is fully aware that he is perfectly capable of any evil. The potency is in all. More than potency. Also the practice, the degree often enough being limited only by good fortune, good luck, and the grace of God.

One had best not enter into that wasteland without being armed with the Gospels. It is precisely in them that Christ is portrayed as mercy incarnate come to save man from his hidden darkness.

You can learn a great deal on a motorcycle. For that matter, you can learn anywhere. Life is all mystical. There is another dimension to everything. All things can speak to us of God. That often enough they do not is because we do not permit them to. Do not want them to.

We complain about the darkness, yet will not light one candle lest we see what sort of creatures we are. We prefer illusion. Yet, to live with illusion is not to live at all. In any case, the truth we will not see within us will inevitably take shape before our eyes in the world around us. The chaos and disaster we refuse to acknowledge within will thus take revenge on us and become evident everywhere.

The Redeemer of the world walks unheeded our trafficked highways, unseen, unrecognized. No one needs a Redeemer. It's as simple as that. If they needed him, they would see him, for even the blind know his presence. They do not need him because they are not real and live in an unreal world, divorced from the truth. In an unreal world, reality does not exist.

So to live is not to live, for it is to live without love. The divine life within has never been known. The dark monsters that hide his presence are not faced, are not overcome. One lives in fear and dread of the truth, one is not free. In which case, never get on a motorcycle.

9.

The Monastic Influence

Most people do not think of seminaries as monasteries, but there are very real similarities, for monastic influence has made a deep impression on Catholic life. The prayer of the diocesan priesthood has long been similar to that of monks, if not identical, even though recited privately and not in choir. It was not long ago that parish churches had Vespers, and cathedrals often had a divine office similar to that of monks, sometimes sung by monks or the near equivalent. Perhaps the priest's cassock is derived from the cowl or robe.

The seminary in which I was educated for the missionary priesthood was in many ways like a monastery. In fact, when I entered Gethsemani, I found the similarity striking. In certain ways, in fact, the seminary was more of a monastery; there we had our own wheat fields, ground our own flour, made

our own bread. We had a huge herd of milk cows and
steers and hence our own butter and beef. We smoked
our own sausage, bacon, ham. We had a large apiary
and always had honey on the table. We had a large
poultry farm and a set of shops for electrical,
mechanical, and woodworking projects. If we did not
have monastic enclosure, we had a reasonable
facsimile. In my eight years there I was home for my
father's funeral and my first Mass, seventy-two hours'
leave in each case, and received one visit from my
sister and one from my brother. We had our share of
silence and seclusion. So there were similarities. The
monks at Gethsemani had, in fact, long since given up
their mill and their chickens, and their milk went for
cheese.

Years later, when renewal came about, many
seminarians were explicit in their desires to shed
monastic influences, insisting quite rightly, I think,
that they were not monks and were not meant to be.
Neither are diocesan priests, though, like monks,
they are celibate.

It is the question of celibacy, monastic life,
seminaries, that interests me. I rather suspect that a
flaw in seminary life, as I knew it, was not that it was
monastic, but that it was not monastic enough, or not
monastic in the right way. I would say the same of
diocesan seminaries.

It seems to me that seminaries have copied
monastic observance and have suffered from the same
omission as do monasteries: the lack of emphasis on
solitude.

Certainly the measure of solitude to which some

diocesan priests are exposed is a great deal more than the average monk knows. Many priests live alone. In the case of the missionary, he knows double solitude, since he not only often lives alone, but in a foreign land, an exile.

When seminaries did not pick up the solitary note in the monastic tradition, they perhaps missed what was most necessary, most useful. It is a difficult thing to live alone. One needs to be educated to it. I think few seminarians receive such help. Most priests seem to know little of the spiritual aspects of solitude, and I know that for missionaries, solitude is a very serious problem.

If the monastic life, especially through Merton, has recently begun to rediscover the values of solitude, perhaps seminaries ought to look into the matter as well. It is best to talk simply. If a young man has a passionate interest in women, he usually does not enter a seminary or a religious order. The idea does not enter his head. If the idea does come, we may assume that marriage does not strike him as essential to his happiness. All things are possible, so perhaps by reason of his milieu or his upbringing, the state of his mental health, or some romantic disaster, a man may venture into the celibate state with inadequate attitudes. It will be best for him if he is not accepted, or later discouraged from continuing, if he does not come to that conclusion himself. It would seem, though, that the usual candidate for the celibate state feels that for the love of God he could forego marriage.

This may perhaps mean that the presence of the anima within him is already so strongly manifest that

he does not feel the need for an actual relationship
with a woman in order to reach wholeness. There
have always been such men, and I suppose there
always will be. Often enough, it is among them that a
culture will find its poets, its artists, its dreamers, its
prophets, priests, seers. In a sense they are a breed
apart, but in another sense they are a figure of the man
to come, since they already have an initial grasp of an
integrity that is humankind's destiny, that union of all
forces in ourselves that makes us truly one. Every
person is called to such an inner wedding, but to some
it is a call to work out that union with Christ, not by
physical love, but by mystical.

This is not an easy road to walk and it is full of
dangers. Further, one needs counsel and inspiration
in following it. Hermits learned early the wisdom of
converse with a holy elder experienced in the ways of
the heart, and monks soon joined one another in
fraternal love the better to sustain the solitary
endeavor. Yet, solitude remains the core experience,
and one called to this state, no matter what the
external circumstances, will always feel himself
somehow as one apart and probably knows it has
always been like that.

Yet in an age as opposed to the feminine as our own,
such a person faces formidable difficulties. If we are
the products of an environment that stresses reason,
law, order, science, achievement, agression, violence,
self-assertion, organization, institution—there the
anima is going to be driven deep and even beyond
reach. What sort of person or what sort of culture this
leads to we need not imagine, since we have only to

look around us, but for the one called by God and apparently by nature to the inner union, the problems are real and immediate. The society that has small regard for woman is no help at all for the man trying to come to terms with her within himself.

By reason of an inner experience of the feminine, he may sense no exceptional longing for physical union with a woman, and still be at a loss to know what to do with his own being. In a sensuous age he may simply drift into sexual union with his own kind, particularly if he is exposed to this before he has had adequate time to understand himself. It is no great grace to know too much too soon.

If the mystic dimension has all but vanished from our world, where are such men to turn? For it is to the mystic they are called. And the mystic has also nearly vanished from the church. The monastic life itself, nurturing ground for the mystical life, often turns to practical matters like education and missions, emphasizes prowess in farming or in marketing products, or expresses itself in arduous labor, grim discipline, or a difficult interpretation of the rule.

The scene is changing, to be sure. Merton certainly helped change it. There must needs be some rediscovery of the mystical, and solitude is a basic factor in that discovery. Yet one scarcely hears it given that much emphasis in monasteries, still less in the education of priests for congregations and societies or the dioceses of the church. The figurative espousal of priest to church is passed over.

Yet, it remains important, if difficult. Even in the contemplative life one senses that fresh attitudes and new approaches may fall wide of the mark and settle for more genial communities, less challenging demands, and a somewhat unconscious or instinctual avoidance of solitude. Fear of woman is not unknown to man, and the contemporary prevalence of the strong woman is small help, for a consequent rise of gentle men will produce those who tend to lean on her rather than meet her and relate fruitfully to her. It is necessary to be a man to begin with, yet if man does not relate to woman he cannot develop. Man simply cannot live without woman.

Solitude is no easy answer, but it is a way to an inner dialogue that man eventually must enter into if he is to become a person, one capable of great love.

Merton was pleased by the monks' moving into private cells built where the open dormitories used to be. They provide privacy, quiet. His overall impact on the monastery could likely be summed up in that: the place is quieter. It is true, the concept of silence is less rigid, there is dialogue and discussion, responsibility for material wealth, and a great deal less frenzy over work and production. Some concern for communal love is perhaps undeveloped, but there can be no doubt the monastery is a center of peace and of joy. With access to the woods and fields, with a scattering of little refuges and huts, there is ample scope for times of solitude, and Father Louis's former hermitage is regularly used for longer periods of retreat. All this is directly linked to innerness, and given time will manifest itself in a depth of charity and compassion, tolerance, and a spirit of prayer.

Once a man has passed through his own inner

darkness and moved on to the realm of the bride within, his sense of identity with the human family must be so intense that his very presence should convey it. To such a journey we are called, and called in particular are they who respond to the celibate life. These are the poets of the human family. They sing our love songs. What is more important than that a people have singers of songs, men gifted with magic words and mystic insights lest the rest of us famish along the way?

Currently, some experiments are being conducted in new modes of both seminary study and seminary life. I know little of them, but there does seem a less intense community life, greater personal responsibility, genuine commitment to study. That the young are thrown much more on their own, must face issues and work out solutions, manage their lives — this is in the direction of solitude.

Bonhoeffer sometimes makes disparaging remarks about monasticism, yet when he was entrusted with the training of a group of seminarians, he gathered them in a small remote setting and established them at Finkenwalde in a community of prayer, work, and study that was very much a monastery. By reason of his influence on them and the quality of the life they lived, the period proved to be a rich spiritual experience for all concerned. These influences of meditation, silence, seclusion, in a framework of a fraternity of love and worship, were as profound as in any real monastic community and remained with the participants all their lives. This experiment deserves attention and may indicate precisely what was originally intended in the modeling of seminary training in the Church on the monastic style of life, where monastic observance is not enough, or even required.

A few years ago I briefly visited the seminary where I had been educated; it was just prior to its transfer to a university campus and the men had been involved that season and some seasons previously with a form of controlled-environment encounter in which small groups tried to help one another discover his own truth.

At the time I could not help admiring their courage. As a monk I could understand what they were doing, though, as I told them, the method seemed harsh and perhaps dangerous, even if some profited much from it. The monk's method is slower, more gentle, but the end result is the same, at least at that stage. The monastic ascesis would lead one to a knowledge of the truth, the beginning of all growth in the spirit. Certainly the awareness these young men had of the need to know their own truth, the price they were willing to pay for it, says a great deal.

One hopes they can continue further, not merely in finding new and effective ways to truth, but also into the mysteries of solitude and the life of prayer. Perhaps some students of Jung could help them. The question of celibacy is discussed often on too shallow a level, and surely so if the mystical level is dismissed. To do that is to reduce celibacy to an act of prowess which as likely as not can end only in ruining the man. Celibacy without a deep love affair is a disaster in a priest. It is not even celibacy. It's just not getting married. And the world has enough such men, married and otherwise.

10.

Psalmody

It is a great pity that psalmody has all but disappeared from the life of the Church. Beyond some monks and nuns who chant the psalms and the use of psalms in the prayer of priests, these prayers seem not much in use save for a certain role in the Eucharist. One could hope for a return to this form of prayer, if for no other reason than its special appropriateness for our own times.

After the Our Father, we have no finer prayers. They are, to begin with, part of Scripture and therefore the word of God. Their use through Christian centuries and back into the days of the Old Law is a sort of perduring note that continues to be heard into our own time, even if more feebly. A return to the psalms is a return to deep prayer, scriptural prayer, human prayer.

The fright that people sometimes experience on picking up the psalter and uttering its words may perhaps express a kind of naive understanding of the human heart's mysteries. The psalms strike one with their frankness, their passion, their dipping into violence and wildness. Put side by side with what we think of as fitting forms of prayer, they appear primitive and extravagant, removed from the restraint and measure of the Our Father, the Hail Mary, the Magnificat, or the Benedictus.

Sometimes even monks are shocked at the language of the psalter and go so far as to delete what they feel to be inelegant verses, indeed, even to passing over whole psalms. They find the words out of place in their mouths. Many would join them in this attitude and prefer to think of the psalms as an interesting form of ancient religious poetry, but one ill-suited to contemporary man. Others dismiss them airily as simply not Christian and consequently not proper to our spiritual life as the followers of Christ. Yet, if the psalms are not Christian, it must be remembered that our hearts are not either, certainly not wholly. And granted even that our hearts be totally imbued with Christ and his spirit, it remains that the Lord himself used the psalms in prayer and commended us to look to them if we would learn of him.

I would suppose our lack of contact with the landscape of our own hearts leads us to assume that the psalms are not pertinent. Yet, if the world scene is so much one of chaos and fright, this scene is but a revelation of the heart of man and its fruit.

If we listen to our dreams, if we remain still in the

dark of night, if we are available to the evidence that rises from deep within us in moments of quiet, of pondering, not to say hours of anguish or sudden grief, we must conclude that any assumption that innocent tranquility is the character of the heart is unfounded.

In our own heart's depth we touch not merely a capacity for total good and total evil, but in some way, too, reach the whole heart of mankind and all that courses through it. It is perfectly true that all humankind lies hidden in the depths of every human being.

Yet this contact with total reality, our own and the human family's, is not something everyone is willing to make or to endure. It is understandable. Generally we have had enough to do with evil in our own lives to make us extremely wary about further evidence in that direction. Further, we may have so structured some sort of style, a set of things done and not done, that we are not able to risk this flimsy make-do in the face of what seems to be overpowering or even inimical forces. In fact, we may earnestly consider it our moral duty to avoid doing so.

The result of such living, however, may lead only to an artificial, brittle total that both we and others vaguely sense to be somehow unreal. And this sentiment may lead us to even more staunch efforts to hold our own.

This may be living, but it is not a way that makes real prayer a possibility. Prayer is rooted in reality. If we are screened from reality, our prayers are bound to be formulas. And since prayer is a form of love, it is not too much to say that in such a manner of life even love is inhibited and stifled, despite sentimental icing.

The peculiar lack of compassion and mercy that is often a quality of a good man may stem from this situation. If I do not know myself truly, then I take for my reality what I choose. The choice may be excellent and impressive, but it cannot possibly last, for it is but stage scenery.

When a person given to living on a stage set is offered the psalms for personal prayer, his reaction can only be one of alarm, perhaps hidden by irritation or boredom, for a cagey instinct will warn him. The psalms walk backstage at once.

The psalms, prayed with Christ, can lead us to the truth and in the truth to freedom. The road to freedom is a good road, but it is not always pleasant going. It ends on the hill. There is true death in the act of becoming born free, just as there is true resurrection made possible in the rising of Christ. It is no small matter to look on as one's dreams and illusions are shattered, one's carefully erected setting demolished by an expert in a few deft moves. An empty stage and an empty theater become some great chasm full of the echoes of past make-believe. So seems our heart then.

Nor is that all. For the very theater which is our world is not merely empty and hollow, but its actual fabric begins to fall apart before our eyes, exposing us to the whole universe. We are totally overwhelmed by the outer darkness, nor is there any place to hide, for it is a darkness of penetrating light and insight. Our reaches are infinite, our capacities without limit. One stands nude before God, knowing he knows.

That is the reason we must always pray the psalms with Christ; or better, let him pray them in us. With him we can oppose the powers of darkness and evil, with him walk the way of God's will, with him pray to the Father for the triumph of good in my heart and every heart.

Until I have some hint of the inner scene, any exchange with my neighbor is bound to be shallow. I can reach only that depth in him that I can reach in my own spirit. If my self-perception is artful and hedgy, so will my hedginess approach his heart. It follows, too, that I will sense immediately when someone sees more deeply into me than I do, and will fly to my defense with vigor, a defense usually made effective by counterattack. Yet, once I come to accept the truth and join the human family, the futility of mutual sparring and jockeying becomes evident. It seems pointless to be determined to manifest superiority, to search out weakness, to take advantage of lapse and slip. Compassion is born only of my own passion, not another's. It is not to be had otherwise. Only those who have been ill can speak the healing word. If you do not know how it feels, this lack will be glaringly evident to one who does. And this has nothing to do with achievement, accomplishment, superb prowess. It is much more negative than that. Much more passive. It is something you let happen to you rather than do. It is a submission to truth.

It is precisely in this climate of truth and reality where we savor the poverty and frailty of man, his guilt, his capacity for evil, that we come to understand

Christ as Redeemer and Savior. Christian life then begins.

It is good to pray the psalms. It is good to pray all of them, in order as they occur, for the moods of the psalms are more varied even than our own, come home more readily when we do not seek to match their tone to ours. In the small monastery in Carolina we used to read the psalms aloud, slowly, quietly. One read; the others sat still and listened. After a few minutes, another would continue with the next psalm, and so on. We read the whole psalter in the course of a week, one psalm after the other, dividing them roughly into three portions for each day; a generous one for the middle of the night, one at sunrise, one at sunset.

Dawn and dusk are obviously fitting times for prayer, marking the beginning and the end of creation, of time, of life. The night has long been favored as uniquely suited for prayer, for making love. And let not the place be too brightly lit, for one should be aware of the dark, the stars, and of the wind, mystery. Do not make a project of it. Perhaps it is better to let the psalms speak as they may; we should merely voice them. In time, we discover that we ourselves are speaking through these poems, or more aptly, that Christ is praying them with us, in us. Sometimes our heart is not quite in it. No matter, one keeps on. The heart will catch up later on.

At the monastery we used to add a portion of reading from the Scriptures; from the Old Testament at night, from the New during the day. Again, we took the books and Gospels and letters as they came, reading as much as seemed to make a coherent selection. It is good to hear Scripture read aloud, all of it, or to do it alone if one's prayer is solitary. And to understand the significance of our spiritual journey, nothing is better than going through the pages of the Old Testament, while as Christians, we cannot live without communion with Christ's word. It is especially the Gospels that explicate the psalms.

The earliest monks spent a great deal of time with the psalms. As monastic life flourished, as communities developed, so did styles of reading and chanting the psalter. Eventually, antiphonal singing of the psalms by facing choirs became customary, the psalms lending themselves without difficulty to this practice since they are poetry and often express their ideas in couplets. The quality of the accompanying chant was long known for its spirituality. With the passage of centuries, many elaborate additions were made, in music, attire, ritual, to produce a total action of impressive nobility, which for all its art may perhaps have somewhat muted the vigor of the basic ingredient: the psalms. Even when reduced to a barren reading done quietly and humbly, one wonders if the psalms do not strike home more directly. Let be. It is the psalms that matter, their use. Let contemporary art achieve, if it can, some manner of adapting the psalms to community use in one form or other. It would be a great service to the Church.

One could do worse than lead the people back to the psalter. We all need wisdom in the mysteries of the human heart; the very fact that the psalms have been so long with us indicates that they may have something to teach us. In the face of so much chaos, disruption, and confusion, perhaps men are beginning to suspect that most things happen first in the heart, have their source and font nowhere else. The psalms are nothing if not prayers of the heart, and thus the heart's salvation.

11.

The Destroying Angel

Who is this dark demon that pursues me? Who sent him? Why does he haunt me? Who can this enemy within be, and why has he chosen to destroy me?

I wish I knew. I know only that he has been around as long as I can remember. He sees deep into me and by his own mean insight determines with swift certainty just where and just when to strike.

Where would he lead me? Over what sudden precipice would he have me leap? Or slip? What is the scope of his designs, since he acts, be it secretly, or now that I am better acquainted with him, openly, for familiarity with him has given no indication whatever as to what his next tactic will be?

It is not so much that I fear him; he wears me down. He does not so much hurt me as hover over me like some wheeling vulture waiting his right moment.

What is it about man that turns him on himself?
Where did I learn this black art? Somewhere,
somehow, I discovered I was hateful and therefore
that hate was called for. They loved me; I know that.
Who then skilled me so? Perhaps I learned early that
man is devious and far from God, that the good angel
in me gave offense to the evil one.

As a child I used often to go sit in the woods on the
little hill back of the house. The woods were birch and
the quality of the leaves in spring, their scent, the play
of sunlight on me, on them, the grass, the streaked
white curls of bark—none of this has ever left me.

And do you know what I used to do there? (I do not
remember seeing anyone do it, for my mother was no
woman with a needle, but I must have observed it
somewhere.) I used to take a linen napkin from the
buffet in the dining room, get colored thread and
needle, and then trace in stitches the patterns
embossed on the fabric or woven into it. The process
fascinated me and I am sure I spent hours quietly
tracing the whorls and whirls of the fanciful designs.
It was a delight. And I remember consciously
thinking, and I must have done so many times, that
the world was very beautiful, but that people were
not. I felt the world would have been so fine a place
without them. I sometimes feel now that I was onto a
truth, though I was yet to learn that I was people.

My father provided my sister and me with a tent
mounted on a platform under a huge elm. We were not
encouraged to play with other children in their yard,
nor to have them come play with us. There were few
children in the neighborhood anyway, so it did not

much matter. Only later did we venture. But in those early years I spent much time by myself and have never lost the sense of charm that surrounded those days. Sometimes I would sit by myself in the tent, drawing or making a scrapbook of pictures scissored from magazines. Now and then my mother would come and get me, asking me to go to the store or telling me we were going for a ride, and I would drop everything and leave. Yet I always felt it a pity I had to, and sensed clearly enough that she was a little distressed at the way I was.

Once when I was very little, I was sitting on the floor of the porch with my back up against the wall. My mother was nearby. I began hitting the wall with the back of my head, not really hard, but hard enough to feel it and recognize that the wall was harder than my head. My mother looked at me as I kept it up and in a sort of pity, with alarm in her voice, told me to stop it. I clearly recall my reaction: she thinks there is something wrong with me, silly woman.

I liked being by myself; I always have. The early years were quiet and untroubled. When school days began, a whole new field opened up. I do not know whether we were actually taught it, whether I picked it up, whether it came from within, but I developed a quality of aggression, strife, contention that was ugly. From then on and for years I was streaked with something vicious. By myself, one sort of person; with others, often enough, quite another. I was dreadful.

Yet, I had friends who meant much to me and I knew deep affinities, though these too were marred with the same blight. Over the years a consciousness began to develop in me that I was different, that I felt things differently, responded differently. This was not accompanied by any feeling of inferiority, nor did I feel superior, but felt sure of myself, felt good in my own eyes.

I believe I was nearly in high school before I entertained any sense of inadequacy. There were some friends of the family with children the age of my sister and me with whom we sometimes exchanged visits. We all got on well. Once after my sister had come back from several days' visit with them, she told me that Mrs. H did not like me. Looking back, I sympathize with Mrs. H's point of view, but at the time it gave me a great shock that someone would not like me. I had always assumed everyone did and that they had some reason to. It bothered me for a long time.

The three aspects have lasted all through the years. I am now nearly sixty and sense just as keenly now as I did then, that there are no delights like the delights of solitude; all my life I have been contentious, full of strife, argument, sarcasm, ridicule; I have never really doubted that I had a destiny and that my gifts were real.

The only shift has come in the last years since 1960 when I became a monk. I was forty-five then. The fruit of my monastic experience has been a shedding of the love for contention. The whole shell of outer strife was exposed as a construct, and under the impact of grace, guidance, the monastic milieu, it simply disintegrated. Though it sometimes may still express itself, I know what is going on.

For one thing, I am not a natural fighter. Fight to me has always seemed silly and pointless. You were either right or you were wrong. Violence did nothing to change anything. Yet, I believe that in a society of competition, in a setting of achievement, striving, aggression, I either learned or was taught that fighting is part of the scene. So I learned, but in my own way. Since it was not natural to me, the results were disastrous.

The same applied to sports. I did not lack endurance, or courage, or ability to bear pain. I loved to ice-skate, to ski, to swim, to go sledding, to build tree houses; I enjoyed simple games, long hikes, bicycling. But the idea of organized play, with winning and losing and all that was involved, simply did not interest me. I saw no point in any of it. Even in going to motion pictures as a child, I used to be appalled at the wild exhibitions of glee or hatred for hero or enemy, which would burst from the audience with such intensity. I felt sure I grasped as much as did the others the impact of good and evil, but to lose one's self in such mass hysteria seemed something I neither wanted to do nor could do.

Sometimes I wished I were more like others. I am aware of a difference, some insight into things, some capacity for the poetic and the spiritual which, if not exceptional—and it is not—is still strong enough to set me off from others. Nor do I hesitate to say that this has some relationship to homosexuality, for though I have never practiced it, I am well aware of an orientation that is certainly as much in that direction as the other; further, that given the knowledge, the opportunity, the circumstances, I could as easily as not have gone in that direction. But people of my kind seem often so placed; the reason, as I have worked it out, being that they are more closely related to the anima than is usual and thus have far less need of the actual woman. What such people yearn for is solace in their solitude and an understanding of their fate, their destiny. I do not think a homosexual relation would be much of an answer. The man with a strong anima will always sense some inadequacy until he has come to terms with his inner spirit and established communion—no small achievement. Until then he cannot really act truly as a complete person, since he isn't one. He will thus be unable to relate in depth to others. The unhappy experience of many is that they cannot relate to others, not aware that the problem is their lack of communication with themselves. The blind comfort the blind, but they cannot open each other's eyes. True, a relation may release sexuality and in a sex-impressed context there may be no other way, just so one does not mistake one thing for something else. Perhaps a healthy culture would enable those so gifted by God or nature to realize their call and respond to it in fruitful ways. Our times seem not unusual for homosexuality; we are perhaps more self-conscious, have more contempt of the feminine, and have less reverence for the gift of insight than is good for us.

Yet, now that I have at last shed the veneer of acquired aggression, I have discovered a hidden monster I was not aware of before. Now he has turned his face on me. There is to the anima a companion sister who seems full of venom, spite, and the spirit of destruction. She is an evil woman who attacks the good anima with hell's fury, and for those endowed with a strong relation to the anima, this can mean only trouble.

It cannot have escaped anyone with even a casual knowledge of artists, poets, actors, writers, dreamers, and, I may add, men and women of religion, how their lives are often marked with and sometimes destroyed by disasters which often enough are of their own making. It does not make light reading, this study of the biographies of these gifted people that reveal so much suffering and sorrow, and, unaccountably, too often self-inflicted.

A destroying angel is near every poetic soul. Humble though my own gifts be, I am none the less more than conscious of a self-destructive urge that is active within me. I have repeatedly discovered myself having done things inevitably bound to bring rebuke, refusal, contempt, rejection. In a word, I ask for these things, unconsciously, unwittingly. I set things up that way. The only solace following the certain consequences is knowing that for a while, at least, the hunger of the destroyer is sated.

Why this is so, I do not know, but I know it is so. I do not think success for an artist would be any help. Indeed, it might lead only farther into the abyss, for the more his gift be praised, the stronger the enemy. Probably the only real answer lies in religion, in deep faith in God's love and mercy. But even deep faith does not necessarily solve all life's problems. Salvation, yes, but not necessarily happiness on earth. Yet, I do believe that faith is the greatest help against this demon.

If God has made a gift to me, there is no reason I should hate myself for being so gifted. Unless I happen to know I am unworthy; and then? Then you turn to Christ, aware that we are all unworthy, even of life itself; and acknowledging unworthiness and the forgiveness of all sin by his merciful death, we can resist the enemy.

It is good to think sometimes that if people who seem blessed with special gifts are yet unspeakably difficult, resentful, cantankerous, jealous—that this may be the only way they can release the venom of the evil angel within. Or, in more tragic situations, when an artist soul turns self-destructive, others should be compassionate. Great gifts attract demons.

Of late years contemplative monasteries are updating a lot of customs and traditions. In former days the abbot was simply head of the monastery and ran the place as he liked, more or less, according to the Rule of St. Benedict, the prescriptions of the Order, and an occasional rebuke or reminder by the visitator. The beneficial side was that monks were spared administrative duties, meetings, boards, reports. Now that the atmosphere is gone very democratic, many more areas are open to the monks. This has led to interminable meetings, dialogues, discussions, and almost endless wrangling trying to come to a consensus or even a majority on some issues. Monks have long since expressed exasperation. Further, the sudden call from a life of silence to a life of exchange, of opinion expressed in public, of voting, of argument that sometimes becomes emotional or personal—all this has made evident the fact that monks are not exactly skilled in this sort of thing. The general assumption has been that having had nothing to say for so long, they simply lost the art of speaking. Monks find it difficult to express themselves, get angry, get upset. In the face of that, most agree more dialogue is called for, more discussion, until they get used to it, get good at it.

I wonder about that. In fact, I suspect it's all wrong. I'll venture a prophecy: that monks will return to the old way and let the abbot take care of most things, and submit only a few basic concerns to vote or discussion by the community—just about the way it used to be.

Because monks by and large are artists, poets. They are heavy with anima, sons of strong mothers. They are romantics, idealists, dreamers. They must be. If they were practical men of affairs they would have gone out and done something more useful than chant psalms in the night, spend a lifetime making cheese for Christ's sake.

If they are anima men, you can be sure they know the dark demon of destruction. And if they do, you can guess them generally hopeless in the give and take, the strife, contention, and controlled aggression that is essential to a good community discussion. I am sure most of them hate the whole business. They'd sooner suffer the whims of an abbot (they are all whimsical) than bear the venom of their own and another's abysmal spirit.

We'll see.

In monastic life, submission to the abbot is central, and for the kind of man called to the monastery, that form of discipline is superb, for he needs a firm hand. Not a hand that crushes him, but protects him from the forces that fight against him, his own self-destroying urges.

The same may be said of the monastery as a whole, for it forms an enclave of peace and of love in which elements that could only destroy are kept at bay. This means that the monastic enclosure does not keep the monk in; it rather keeps the enemy out, the evil one, the spirit of violence. When that is the situation, then the battle is centered where it should be, in the heart. External hostility is mere distraction for the monk, leads him away from his center, dissipates his energy in externals. His warfare is within, and, let it be noted, a more deadly combat than anything without.

It follows, then, that the introduction of fields for contention and provocation simply introduce an element that can do the monk no real good.

When the poet, the artist, the writer, must spend his time fending, fighting off critics, earning a living, contending with any external forces, that can mean only a dissipation of his own gift. A heaven of peace does not mean he is spared conflict; it means the conflict is centered when the real enemy is met, not a stand-in.

The destroying angel that accompanies every man of the spirit is a real danger. Mere intellectual grasp of the concept will not do. Neither can will power avail. It is a matter mostly of prayer, a wrestling with demons with Christ and in his grace.

Not a few monks leave the monastery because of the destroying angel. He drives them out; I am quite certain of that. Not all of them, to be sure, for some should leave. But when a human approaches God, the enemy has a way of capitalizing on the utter unworthiness of the lover to the point that the lover cannot abide it. One needs a sort of compassion for poets and priests and artists. We do not realize what a precious gift they are to mankind. Or what a burden they bear.

When I began to experience the call to solitude, and to solitude away from the monastery, I was wary of the destroying angel and feared he might be deluding me. It was for that very reason I insisted that I would never leave without the abbot's blessing. When my abbot did refuse his blessing, it hurt me, but I had no great difficulty in accepting it. This was not virtue, but common sense. Monks get carried away with all kinds of ideas. Several years later a new abbot did give me his blessing. This confirmed me more strongly in my faith in obedience as the foundation of monastic discipline. It is this sort of death in the will of God that at once unites the monk with Christ before the Father and puts to flight the evil one. Yet, it is not always easy. They did not name the place Gethsemani for nothing.

12.

The Virgin

Sad in the Church of our time is the weakening of
devotion to the Virgin Mother of God. Does it indicate
a disintegration of the faith? Is it a portent of chaos to
come? Perhaps the only hope one can express is that in
the loss of reverence for our Lady in accustomed
forms, new modes may develop from the depths of the
Christian heart. Certainly not all devotion is genuine,
nor its forms appropriate to every age.

I knew a bishop who prided himself on his love for
the Virgin Mary, led pilgrimages, named every new
parish in his diocese after one of her titles, yet, not
withstanding, was rather cruel and hard-hearted.
Precious little in him reflected the tenderness of
Christ's Mother.

Perhaps loss of love for the Virgin is part of an
overall rejection of woman that has been characteristic
of this and recent centuries. A casual survey of the

state of woman today gives one no great comfort. For all its forms, the movement for the liberation of woman may at least be taken as some sort of effort to restore her dignity.

We now know in full measure the fruit of long neglect of the human heart. In a world ridden with violence and turmoil, so accustomed to wars of unequaled scope and ferocity that we take them in our stride, we grow adjusted even to a life subject to global annihilation at any moment. In such a world to talk of the Virgin Mary is to be brave indeed.

Yet talk of her we must, and we must return to her somehow or other. The poverty of Protestantism in regard to our Lady is acknowledged, yet we face becoming an equally womanless faith. And, may it be said, a religion without woman is no religion at all.

No man is only male. The human race is not just male. How can we relate to God without reference to woman? God is as much male as female. And how can we come to know the whole Christ if we have no woman through whom to do so? And to assume that we can relate to the Church, our mother, Christ's spouse, without the model, his own holy Mother, is to imagine that mere formulas and concepts are realities.

Woman can mean very little to man if he has no contact with the feminine spirit within him. And woman herself, sensing this rejection and misunderstanding, will surely turn against herself. When woman means little to man, the Virgin Mary will also mean little, and a relationship to the church will have no real depth without her influence.

Carl Jung maintained that the most significant

event of our times was the proclamation of the doctrine of the Assumption of the Virgin Mary. He saw it as such because it expressed the reality of the Virgin and the reality of woman's role in the plan of God in the face of a world that spurns the body, the Resurrection, and woman. He could think of nothing the world needed more and so rejoiced in it. So astute an observer of the human spirit deserves respect. Nor was he given to making statements lightly. He was convinced that because man was divorced from his own spirit, his own depths, all that he rejected would take its revenge on him and confront him in wild fury from without. He does not seem far wrong. Spurned woman is lethal.

No man will have any serious affinity to the Virgin Mary who does not have a serious affinity to woman. One is impossible without the other. For a Christian of the Catholic tradition, one could almost judge his understanding of woman by his devotion to the Mother of God.

Sometimes we are annoyed at the forms devotion takes, the esthetic quality of shrines, works of art, various practices. We could use some help. Yet, there are many lovely expressions to be had, and reproductions of the finest work in the world can be acquired easily enough. Nor are new works lacking. Even many old prayers are beautiful. The litany of Loretto is scarcely heard anymore, yet it is rich in imagery of a superior kind. The parish of my childhood was no more than a grubby basement-church utterly without presence. May devotions consisted of a layman reciting the litany of Loretto while the priest was offering Mass. One could scarcely do less. Yet those melodious titles rolling out one after another have always remained vivid in my memory, even if the only bit of loveliness accompanying them was a ray of morning sun streaking color across the cool darkness.

Certainly the years in the seminary were marked by all kinds of devotional practices to our Lady, some of them marked more by sentiment than by faith, yet saying something. An evening May procession with tapers to the Lourdes grotto was not lacking in picturesque qualities, nor have passing years substituted anything better. Yet, recalling past days and bemoaning the present serves small good. It must be confessed that a certain disenchantment, hard to shake, has settled on our spirits. Yet, if the faith lives, love of the Virgin will again flourish.

What a long time ago seems the gathering that overfilled Soldiers' Field in Chicago for the Marian year. It was a most effective work of organization, and I found it deeply moving. It was a cool summer evening with a light breeze off the lake, as I recall, and the great crowd was extraordinarily reverent, the thousands of candles burning in the dark stadium a sight not lacking in message.

Perhaps the day of such innocent pageantry and display is gone. Times are more bitter, the heart more grieved, and some great darkness has settled in on us, too dark, too somber, to bear the glimmer of little candles, since the darkness is touched with a despair we rather relish. One thinks of the power of darkness.

The National Shrine in Washington is of that bygone era. It seems so prosperous, so happy, so sure.

It does not reflect the mood of the times, since it glows with optimism in an unhappy city and an unhappy land. No matter. Give it time to make history. Let it live with us through these dark days and the days to come. Sorrow and suffering will soften its brilliance and warm its gold. Once it has shared our pain, it will come closer.

In our suffering, too, we shall grow closer to the Mother of God. Nothing softens the heart as does pain. We shall not resist her.

One night at Gethsemani the Brother I used to work with, taking care of the thoroughbreds we boarded then for local stables, came for me. A snowstorm had blown up and he thought we had better go take a look at the back pasture. Normally, these strikingly handsome animals were high-strung, skittish, excitable. In an open field they were not always easy to approach. "If they are in trouble," Brother said, "we'll be able to tell right away." They were in trouble. The wind was high; there was no refuge from it, with their coats already matted with snow and ice, they huddled together and looked most uncomfortable. When they saw us coming, you could sense their gratitude. With no difficulty we took the first two and led them off to the stables, the rest of them following in unusual docility. They were much tamed and sobered by their plight. "Nothing gentle as a horse hurting," Brother remarked quietly.

No one recommends trouble, but it comes, an uninvited guest for whom room must be made. Dorothy Day was once a deeply troubled woman. She had not long before entered the Church and had a

burning desire to serve God and her fellowman. She
had repeatedly been frustrated in trying to find what
work she was to do. She went to the shrine of the
Mother of God—it was but a lower-level church then
—and begged the help of the Virgin, then went back
home to New York. Peter Maurin was waiting for her
and out of that meeting was born The Catholic
Worker, one of the great glories of the Church in this
country. Such prayers, such answers, multiplied
unending times, are what create a center of faith.
Architecture has little to do with it.

Yet, for all our hoping and praying, it is probably to
be admitted that our devotion to the Mother of God
will be marked by the same attitudes we bear toward
woman on earth. When woman is held in reverence,
virginity reckoned beautiful, marriage and mother-
hood honorable, this will reflect itself in our relation
to the Virgin Mother. We have a certain consistency.

A culture capable of combining contempt for
woman with the commercialized gush of Mother's
Day is the same that is distressed by Christ's relation
to his own Mother. The nobility of the few episodes
passed on to us in Scripture manifests a respect of
each for the other as a person that is profound, a
complete lack of prettiness in form, revealing the love
that makes candor not merely possible, but inevita-
ble. They truly speak to one another. That kind of
exchange is so rare among us that we are shocked by it
and hasten to explain that they really did love one
another.

The very difficulty we have in sensing any common
note in the attitude of bishop to diocese as a relation of

husband to wife; or, for that matter, of pastor to parish, indicates that a great deal could be improved. Few relate to the Church as spouse, as bride, as mother, in any evident way. One does not think of hierarchy in the same sense as husband. Yet it is to be so. The Church is Christ's spouse. His bride. He gave himself to death for her. Mary, as Virgin and as Mother, is an image of that Church, virginal and maternal. It comes more easily to us to see the Church as institution and the bishops as presidents or constituting a board of directors. Or put the other way around, I feel considerable sympathy for the woman who is spouse of a bishop.

The age of abortion, divorce, sterilization, can scarcely be an age of reverence for woman. Rather, it is barbarous in this as it is in its love for violence, massive wars, greed, oppression, contempt for human life and human rights. In such a nightmare, a call for devotion to our Lady seems almost pointless. One might as well wring one's hands in the face of a tornado.

Yet she was there when we crucified her Lord. And heard him forgive us. And heard him commend us to her care.

13.

The Company

The galaxies of spirits who surround God's throne and ours are as much a part of my life as wind and rain, dreams and daffodils. People who dispense with angels strike me as among the dullest; I find them no different from men who would as soon as not be deaf, would gladly go blind, cousins to dissolute youth who waste or destroy precious gifts, valuable property, in some false detachment or indifference. Man cannot live without angels; when he does not have them he creates them.

The fancy of a Disney or a Tolkien is not so much mere fruit of creative genius as an intuitive awareness of what grown-up children want most of all; something to believe in. The ability to provide it was theirs. They did very well, though reality is far more fanciful. An angel is no Snow White.

The trend is to cool the angels. This is no great problem, since an age is entitled to its fads and styles. If yesterday's fashions seem ludicrous, yesterday's theological journals are as revealing as old Sears' catalogs. We need not be too much disturbed. Scripture has a certain steadiness; it abounds in dreams and angels.

The glory of the celestial choirs is no more difficult to accept—is it difficult at all?—than one butterfly, one buttercup. Indeed, all creation declares the glory of the angels since with them it praises God and is in the same choir. But the created world, so far as we know, has no conscious voice. What voice the angels have is more glorious for their being conscious in a superior manner.

Creation has been wounded by man's sin and bears part of his guilt. It follows that humankind takes ambivalent attitudes toward the world, reflecting creation's attitudes toward us. The conflict see-saws through time. Plague, famine, flood, fire, earthquake, cyclone—all of them strike at men, now in devastating degree, now less so. Man fights back. Our land is not what it was when we came. The seas and rivers and lakes have been abused. Great treasures have been torn from the earth's breast. The air is no longer pure. We are able to destroy the whole earth if we so want and feel free to do so if we choose.

Man and nature are at war, but not a total war. Much of creation is friendly. And not all people destroy; only some of them, and only more often. The Indians lived here ever so much longer than we have; they seem to have been more kindly to creation. Perhaps they did not take their guilt out on nature as much as we do.

We relate to angels as creation relates to us. Most of our trouble comes from the angels, just as most of nature's trouble comes from us. In the original conflict between good and evil, that great moment of trial and crisis, some angels chose evil. When man's turn came for his love's testing, it was the evil angels who were the agents. Man failed as did some of the angels. He, too, did not love.

It is true, at least in some way, therefore, that we are what we are because of the fallen angels. Had they not come, we would not have joined them in electing evil. But, truly, the fault is not theirs. Our time would have come in any case, fallen angels or not, and we would have chosen our option and taken the consequences. Even so, the angels were associated in what happened to us.

That may explain the particular compassion the good angels have toward us. Apparently there is a vast difference between our fallen state and that of the fallen angels. One gets an impression of something definitive in their fall; no one has said the Redeemer went to them as he came to us. One concludes that they knew better what they did than we, or that their superior qualities made a change of heart impossible. Maybe the story is not ended, more is to come. Yet, since we are redeemable, nature is also, and therefore we look forward not only to the new man, but to the new creation. The whole was redeemed, or better, is being redeemed.

Since the good angels turn to us in love, it seems

only natural to respond. Christian tradition has known many ways of doing so, and like all customs, some of them are exceptionally apt, others less so. Our own age is perhaps unique in dismissing the whole lot.

Will a later age come up with a new understanding of Saint Michael, the archangel, and continue the imagery that surrounds him in icons, statuary, painting, architecture? The oddity of winged humans may or may not be to our taste, though Christian artists have handled the symbol so long and so well that we have long since made it a part of us: when we dream of angels they have wings. One need not, even so, picture angels embodied, or speaking, delivering messages, for as pure spirits they are beyond us.

Many things are. We are familiar with power, energy, influences, waves of various kinds. We do not fully understand them. If angels be conceived as centers of power or light or influence, whose nature is unknown to us, we have at least some point of focus, so long as we realize they are immeasurably superior to anything we know on earth. Their whole being is in the love and the glory of God. We cannot relate to them nor they to us save in those terms.

And those terms are good. We have achieved a great deal. The world abounds in great achievements of man. They give glory to the creative power of God. Yet love is a problem we find difficult to solve. Here we appear at a loss before the power of evil rising in our own hearts, visible in my life and the lives of others, reflected in the retaliation of a world wounded by our malice, our want of love.

Though we know well enough that all love is found

in God, all redemption in Christ, and the total salvation of man and world achieved in him, provided we accept it—we need more.

We need the angels for the same reason we need the Mother of God and the saints—because we are human beings. As human beings we belong to a community. "Contemporary man" is a concept. My neighbor is not. My brothers, my intimates, are real. And we need a wider community than that, for we are not only of this earth. Life is temporary, residence here limited. The trip is a short one, and then we move on to another world, one we have never seen, know little of, have rare reports from. I believe in its existence and my whole life's course is rooted in that, since Heaven is the presence of God. In that presence dwell the angels, forever lost in the beauty which is God. Yet they know me and love me.

So, I have friends in the kingdom, people I know, people who know me. It is not a matter of having influential contacts in high places — unless you prefer it that way — but of being united with their love song, part of it. There is such a song and snatches of it were heard on earth the night Christ was born. Some day that music will be heard again on earth, the day when all will be consummated. Meanwhile we know it continues unending in heaven, the song of love which we are asked to sing with Christ.

14.

Primal Water

Though a son of the Archer and linked to fire, it is to water that I have a more natural leaning. Water is always an invitation to immersion, an immersion with a quality of totality, since it would accept all of me, as I am. Some primal urge invites me to return whence I came.

At times I have done so. There is some special delight in simply walking into a stream, stepping into a lake. The child's delight in a puddle is my adult's in the sea. Come with me down a country road, round a bend to a pond in a meadow, and know the pleasure of turning the motorcycle aside to plunge into the pond with a certain delicious abandon. It is more practical on horseback, for one horse I had was a good swimmer and took to carrying me across deep streams and into cool waters with pleasure, the two of us merged in a common matrix.

No rain falls that I do not at once hear in the sound of the falling water an invitation to come to the wedding. It is rare that I do not answer. A walk in an evening rain in any setting is to walk in the midst of God's loving attention to his earth, and, like a baptism, is no simple washing, but a communication of life. When you hurry in out of the rain, I hurry out into it, for it is a sign that all is well, that God loves, that good is to follow. If suffering a doubt, I find myself looking to rain as a good omen. And in rain, I always hear singing, wordless chant rising and falling.

When rain turns to ice and snow I declare a holiday. I could as easily resist as stay at a desk with a parade going by in the street below. I cannot hide the delight that then possesses my heart. Only God could have surprised rain with such a change of dress as ice and snow. The pines in Carolina, covered with glitter after a night of freezing rain, were ravishing enough to make one overlook the damage, for the display would be costly in broken boughs and backs bent beyond straightening. In Gethsemani snow was rare, but it was not merely its rarity that brought the monks to the door and out into the yard, to stand there wide-eyed for all the white so softly laid. Monks are human. I remember one summer night we had a thunderstorm with splendid rain while we were at compline. Afterward, it was customary then for us all to go to the dormitory; you did not go wandering about. It was evident, as we bowed in turn for the abbot's blessing, that the sun was at work behind the hills, filling the storm clouds above with light and color. I went to my cell and drew the curtain, wishing that I might go up on the roof and see what was going on. I waited a few moments until things were quiet, then slipped out and up the back stairs to the deck above. It was as I expected; the sky was all the fury of the storm turned into color. But I was not alone. There were half a dozen monks there ahead of me, silently taking it all in.

Most people love rain, water. Snow charms all young hearts. Only when you get older and bones begin to feel dampness, when snow becomes a traffic problem and a burden in the driveway, when wet means dirt—then the poetry takes flight and God's love play is not noted.

But I am still a child and have no desire to take on the ways of death. I shall continue to heed water's invitation, the call of the rain. We are in love and lovers are a little mad. The season of love is soon over; one is young but once. It seems a pity that one day I must leave this world, for if I forego rain, I forego much. One of the reasons it is easy for me to believe in a new world, a renewed creation, is that I can scarcely believe God could bring himself to destroy so much beauty. I believe there'll always be rain.

And dew. When I had that happy house beside the lake at Gethsemani, I had to walk through summer fields to reach it. Sometimes it was so rich an experience that I began to suspect it was sinful. The path crossed a small hill, descended through a wooded grove, then over the bottom of a long meadow. Mornings, the tall grass would be leaning over the path with dew, all sprinkled with truly thousands of diamonds so large you could see a rainbow in each. The wood to the left was blued with mist, and inside was cool darkness. I would be wet almost to the waist with such a freshness that I wondered if a shower of dew would not be a remarkable sort. Yet, by the time I would be heading back to the abbey, the sun would be up in the sky, the dew gone, the grass dry, the mist lifted, the woods patterned in sharp light and shadow. Then I would say to myself that I should not get so carried away with passing things.

Bright wintry mornings the temperature would sometimes drop to zero around Gethsemani. When there would be deep snow I would take off to the woods, if the chance came. The land went far in some directions and, even when it led onto neighbors' tracts, continued much a wilderness, deserted. I never met anyone. Sometimes I would go to a glen where I knew the pines were especially fine and not crowded close together. There were wide patches which in summer made quiet secluded havens, but in winter were deep in free-fallen snow. When it was really cold I used to strip quickly and roll in the snow for a bit. In no time the body would react, heat up almost instantly, and one would stand, looking at the brilliant blue above, steam rising from all over one's glistening flesh. One did not wait too long and push it beyond its time, but dress wet as fast as one could. It was a wintry baptism and good for the soul. The only difficulty was the soles of my feet; you could not stand long in the snow, for the heat soon melted it and the feet could not accept the icy water and snow. You had to stand on something else. Then I would head off again and be startled to see a deer dart through the pines. He'd been watching. Probably does the same thing himself, though he no doubt did not bother to kick the snow back over where he'd rolled, as I did.

This is all very droll. I do not go from one thing to another; it is more taking life as it comes. Yet, I must tell you that water is also deep. I have lived close to water all my life and been in and out of it all the time. I have a good relationship with it, but a relationship based on an appreciation of the truth. The pull of water is also a pull backward into that abyss from which we were thrust by a creative force strong enough to prevail. If we are to maintain that creative act, we must not merely abide it, but further it, otherwise life does not catch and we drift back into mother and are absorbed by her, now a devouring primal power, not a life-giving one.

Our touch with water must always take this into account. There is some need to enter her and to unite with her, but if it becomes an absorption, then we have surrendered more than is ours to give and we are lost. Then what poses as love reveals itself as longing for death. This longing has to be renounced and we must face the prospect of being alone, on our own, away from mother.

The same woman who bore me will entice me back, and do so deliberately, happy at once to fail and to succeed; if she fails, a man is born; if she succeeds, she has the pleasure of prevailing. Dominance is the dark side of water.

Drink means little to me except in terms of delirium. I do not need the stimulus from day to day; life itself is so full of spirit that more seems too much of a good thing. Transport is something else. Inebriation appeals to me in any form, for it is what I am born for, what I live for. Any water that will convey me to a sharing in another life I will gladly drink.

Yet it is clear that not every rapture is a preview of heaven or a preparation for it, and then it is a lie. We are called to ecstasy, but in responding we must take note of who is calling. We can be deceived, easily.

No matter how ravenously hungry we be, not everything that passes for good can be eaten. No matter how thirsty, some drink is poisonous. Our spiritual hunger and thirst are more real than bodily; our desires for eternal union in love more powerful than anything temporal. We are deceived when we forget that we are immortal and that our basic longings are infinite.

So life cannot be abandon. One cannot jump in every river, nor dive into every pond. Nor roll in any field. Nor taste every joy. Yet we are tempted to do so, because the calls within us are so very pressing.

I believe I could easily have become an alcoholic. It would require no basic alteration of my shape to lead me that way; I have a perfect disposition for it. I could adjust to it easily, since I have all that longing for primal water, for delirium, for surrender, for rapture. Yet I am aware that I would be walking in the direction of heaven and hell at one time, for I would insist I was seeking the eternal feminine and the divine union even while I knew she was a devouring monster leading to the embrace of extinction.

I am just as aware that I could have moved into a sexual relation with my own kind. It attracts me. I like the idea. It comes naturally. Yet in doing so I would know quite well that it would be a betrayal of that solitude that is basic to my being human, for I would be aware that I needed company in my loneliness, some companion to stand by my side, to assure me he knew how it felt, willing to testify to that by giving me all I had to give him. Yes, and leave me quite as I was before, not one whit less lone.

From early years I knew I had been called by God to priesthood and the celibate life. I sensed the reality and permanence of this vocation as the very being of my life and could not see departure from it as anything less than self-destruction. Christian tradition has been clear in its view on homosexual union: it is to be avoided. Virginal, celibate life by its nature means a union in love which is solitary and does not express itself in sexual commerce; it rejects that mode outright, totally.

There is considerable discussion in this field. I relate it to a basic attitude to the feminine. If I reject the woman within, I simply succumb to the pressure of a common contempt and under its pressure abandon my call to mystical love. On the other hand, as I see divorce and abortion as sins against woman, so also contraception. Though this teaching of the Church is both opposed and ignored, so long as it be her teaching, I accept it, compassionate toward any with problems of conscience in its regard. But to be logical, I do not see that if the sexual act in marriage can be effectively separated from its generative power and used only as an expression of love, why the same act could not be used for love between two of a kind where generation is also not involved. In both cases, a sexual act is used to express love between humans in which generation is or has been rendered impossible. It would appear to me, then, that if one sees birth control licit, he must also concede liberty to homosexual love.

Yet, even if the Church in virtue of new light or fresh insight in the Spirit, declare both of these moral, I would nonetheless continue my chosen path, for it is God's call to me. My road is to be walked alone. My life is within. Virginal love and sexual love are contrary ways.

It is perhaps worth noting, since one at times hears opposite views expressed by those assessing seminary or religious life from the outside and without experience of them, that I found neither in seminary nor monastery anything to foment or express any homoid sexual tendencies. Quite the contrary. If the men following such a state of life are typically, in my view, strongly marked with anima, few of them seem to be positively or obviously drawn to deviance. Further, the life style itself served to slough off into the life stream whatever such tendencies they might have had, as it certainly did in my own case, in a way that not only weakened them, but disposed of them. The ideals of fraternity, love of Christ and the Virgin, dedication to the service of God and one's neighbor, coupled with a life of work and worship, with a strong ascetical emphasis, all combined to create a group of happy men. If I had tendencies that were sexual, in whatever direction, they were absorbed into a love-life of another kind to the point that I was scarcely aware of them in the seminary and less in the monastery. It was rather in the intervening years when there was a less intense communal life, a weakening in prayer and asceticism, together with a not wholly satisfying ministry, that I came to experience a pull I had not formerly been explicitly aware of. For all that, such conditions normally would give stronger voice to sexual desire.

Further, it has been only in the last few years—in my late fifties, be it noted—when living a much more solitary life, that I have come at last to recognize that my trend is real and powerful, and this in a context that is both spiritually vigorous and dynamically rewarding. In other words, exposure to solitude has given me total truth. I can only conclude that the way of life of monks, or religious, is not only a good one, but an excellent one so long as its tone is good, that is, marked by intensity in the mystical, ascetical, communal—solitary aspects. And let only those move on into solitude who are certain God calls them to it, for only then can it be an experience ultimately good. I shall myself continue in it as long as it seems so to me; if I cannot manage, I shall happily return to my abbey.

But I must make clear that I consider religious life, and particularly monastic life as I knew it, an exceptionally fruitful form of life for those called to it. My belief and my hope is that in coming years monastic life, especially of the contemplative kind, will flourish, in that many will find in it a perfect expression of everything they desire. Yet, it is a life of faith, and unhappily, it is precisely faith that is weakening. Without faith monastic life appears weird, and in a sensuous age without faith, even more so. With no such faith, the numbers of men who will not find in monasteries lives of deep meaning and satisfaction will be large enough to be tragic.

Yet there can be no pretending that monastic life is easy. It demands exceptional generosity and a genuine asceticism for Christ's sake, a total acceptance of the virginal, celibate state—the fundamental solitude—with an abandonment of sexual love. Love for the brethren, love for silence, for work and reading, for prayer, for quiet seclusion and peace— all this against a background of unrelenting determination to follow Christ to the end. Christ is no cheap love or easy grace. Though he is mercy incarnate, in obedience to his Father's will he is merciless; that will must be accepted wholly, no matter what it leads to. Sensuality is really not the test of the monk. Obedience is. This obedience leads to death, yet it is a death which in his case, as in ours, is the price of life for us all, the ultimate love.

Since my life has had a quality of journey perhaps some lingering trace of the wandering Celtic monks of ages past—I have come to live the solitary life in New Guinea, the mission world I knew many years ago. Here at my feet is the sea, beating tirelessly against the shore. If we understand one another, the sea and I, it is not an understanding I have always had. I now relive my past in many ways. When I was young and told my mother I was going to study for the priesthood, the reactions were mixed. There was consternation, disappointment, confusion, reluctant acceptance. At no point was there anything like an enthusiastic or encouraging gesture. Nor was there any for many years. I am grateful to her. It was for the best.

I suppose a priest, like a monk, like a prophet, a poet, a dreamer, a solitary, is a jarring note, a disturbing nonconformist voice. Possibly he frightens people. I have been frightened myself. Perhaps if I am too acceptable, to myself or others, I am no help at all.

15.

Easter Sunrise

Holy Week comes to an end, almost entirely spent in noting these reflections, and I come to realize that much of what I have said is not the truth.

It turns out that my elaborate endeavors to detail a pursuit of solitude against opposing elements were no more than an advance disguising a retreat. Flight from woman has been my sin, too. I am a man of my times.

For I have resisted her wooing, have feared her charms, played off her sweet invitations. Now it is clear that it was I who spurned her while making a show of winning her love. The fire I would steal was refused as a gift. I know that now. The elemental truth comes home to me and I see it as it is, yet without regret.

I begin to tell her as we sit on the hill looking out over the sea. She says nothing at all. She smiles softly, takes up my flute and plays a quiet tune, and across

the pipe looks into my eyes. She knows. I know. The
struggle is over and I surrender.

So long a love affair, and yet it could not have been
otherwise. If I had to do it over again, it would be no
different, for I would do the same thing in the same
way. My history is mine and no one else's. Given a
fresh sheet I would write exactly what I wrote the first
time.

I listen to my own song rising from her breath, from
my flute held in her hands. With the rising music the
sun begins to rise out of the sea at her back and there
are no longer two of us. Its light catches the white-gold
ring on my finger.